**This book is from
the kitchen library of**

_____

MR. FOOD®
GRILLS IT ALL IN A SNAP

ALSO BY ART GINSBURG, MR. FOOD®

The Mr. Food® Cookbook, OOH it's so GOOD!!™ (1990)

Mr. Food® Cooks Like Mama (1992)

Mr. Food® Cooks Chicken (1993)

Mr. Food® Cooks Pasta (1993)

Mr. Food® Makes Dessert (1993)

Mr. Food® Cooks Real American (1994)

Mr. Food®'s Favorite Cookies (1994)

Mr. Food®'s Quick and Easy Side Dishes (1995)

Mr. Food®'s Fun Kitchen Tips and Shortcuts (and Recipes, Too!) (1995)

MR. FOOD®
GRILLS IT ALL
IN A SNAP

Art Ginsburg
Mr. Food®

WILLIAM MORROW AND COMPANY, INC.

New York

Library of Congress Cataloging-in-Publication Data ·

Ginsburg, Art.
    Mr. Food® grills it all in a snap / Art Ginsburg.
      p. cm.
    Includes index.
    ISBN 0–688–13711–3
    1. Barbecue cookery. I. Title.
  TX840.B3G55   1995
  641.5'784—dc20   95–7357
                                                            CIP

Printed in the United States of America

First Edition

1 2 3 4 5 6 7 8 9 10

BOOK DESIGN BY MICHAEL MENDELSOHN/MM DESIGN 2000, INC.

Dedicated to
Dad—
My greatest influence

Acknowledgments

What a year this has been! We moved the whole **MR. FOOD®** team into a new home in South Florida, where we can really spread out and have more space to do our "thing"—which is cooking, cooking, and more cooking for my television shows and cookbooks!

The move and this book couldn't have happened without the constant support and incredible perseverance of my family and colleagues. Each of them played a vital part in making it all come together, and I'm extremely grateful to them all.

Once again, I must thank Howard Rosenthal, a man of incredible energy and endless creativity. This book would not have been possible without Howard's input or without the skillful eye of my daughter, Caryl Ginsburg Gershman. She continually pulls together my words and coordinates the creation of my books as "Art"-fully as only she can. My son, Steve Ginsburg, continues to lend all of us his experienced eye, and thanks to the creative input and computer wizardry of Roy Fantel, it was easier than ever to bring together all of this information.

Patty Rosenthal, Alice Palombo, and Monique Drummond have stepped into their new recipe-testing roles masterfully, and none of us would have gotten this far without their comitment to quality.

I wouldn't miss another opportunity to thank my agent, Bill Adler, and my ever-energetic publicist, Phyllis Heller. To my editor, Harriet Bell, and also to Al Marchioni, Skip Dye, Deborah Weiss Geline, Richard Aquan, and Kathleen Hackett, of William

Morrow, and Michael Mendelsohn of MM Design 2000, Inc., I extend more thanks for top-notch work.

As I said before, the "thank-you mat" is out for Ethel, Chuck, Marilyn, Beth, Stacey, Laura, Tom, and my growing family, who are always there to give me the boosts I need. I really appreciate you guys.

My appreciation extends to the following individuals, companies and organizations, too, for their assistance in providing helpful information and product suggestions:

Dairy Management Inc.
Chef Mitchell Fantel of the New York Restaurant School
M. E. Heuck Co.
Jana Brands
Keebler
McCormick®/Schilling®
McIlhenny Company
The National Beef Cook-Off
Propane USA
Tryson House

And, finally, a book on grilling wouldn't be possible without barbecue grills! All the recipes in this book were tested on grills from the following companies:

Thermos
The Ducane Company
Weber Stephen Products Company

Contents

Introduction

Grilling is easy, right? You say you know all about it. After all, people have been cooking over open fires for centuries. Well, that's right. But luckily for us, some things have changed over the years!

Grilling is a quick and easy way to cook, and it's come a long way from the days of starting fires by rubbing two sticks together! There are endless grilling products available today to help us make the best grilled foods. We can choose from charcoal and gas grills and even electric and smokeless grills which have become so popular. And we can grill not only our main dishes now, but every course from our appetizers to our desserts.

I don't know anyone who likes spending hours either preparing food for barbecues or waiting for their food to finish grilling, so don't worry! All you'll find here are recipes that use a few simple ingredients—ingredients that can be found in your local supermarket. (That means no running around looking for fancy products at fancy prices!) And since most of us lead busy lives that leave little time for cooking, these recipes are all fun, quick, easy, and sure to satisfy—and they've been tested and retested so that you won't waste your time and money!

Before you start cooking up my collection of over 130 great grilling recipes, I suggest you start by reading my grilling tips. First there's a section on choosing a grill. After all, that's the first thing you'll need, and you'll want to choose the one that's right for you. Even if you already have a grill, you'll probably want to know about the different sizes, shapes, and types that are avail-

able, from traditional charcoal types—like hibachis and braziers—to the propane and electric grills that fill our stores these days.

Safety should always be our first priority when working near fire and also when preparing food. That's why I've also included safety information important for anyone who works around a barbecue grill, along with tips on the best ways to prepare, serve, and store marinades, meats, and other grilled favorites.

You'll also need to know about the different barbecue accessories that are becoming more available as the popularity of grilling grows. You can choose from a super selection of charcoals and flavored wood chips, long-handled cooking tools, skewers, hinged grill racks, cleaning tools, and more. And something we're never sure of is the best way to put out our charcoal fires and clean and store our grills. Don't worry, there's a section on that, too.

Now don't be afraid to use your grill throughout the year. In cooler climates you may have to extend your cooking times to compensate for cooler outdoor temperatures out of "season," but you should be able to enjoy grilled foods almost year-round.

Okay, with the basics behind you, why not start your barbecued meals off right with some of the fun appetizers I've got here? In **Munchies on the Grill,** there's Mexican Pita Pizza (page 8) and Hot 'n' Spicy Nut Snacks (page 15). After those, you might go for burgers. And I've got a whole chapter for you called **Beyond Basic Burgers.** Of course it includes a recipe for Good Ol' American Hamburgers (page 26), but I also like to make burgers with different twists, like Peppered Turkey Burgers (page 28) and Veal Parmesan Burgers (page 35), and a fun one for the kids, Hamburger "Hot Dogs" (page 30).

Now, what grilling cookbook would be complete without a section on hot dogs? Once you check out the chapter **Hot Diggity**

Dogs and Sausage, Too, you'll never want to eat a plain hot dog again! And, why should you, when you can have Hot Dog Tacos (page 48) and even a complete Breakfast on the Grill (page 46) of sausage, eggs, cheese, and muffins that'll surely wake up your taste buds!

With the popularity of poultry today, I know people are always looking for exciting new ways to make it. In **Charbroiled Chicken Champions,** I've got Chicken Pesto on the Rack (page 77), Grilled Buffalo Wings (page 68), and Ratatouille Chicken Kebabs (page 61). And of course I've got an easier-than-ever recipe for good old Honey-Barbecued Chicken (page 72).

We need our **Mouth-Watering Meats,** too! And there's so much that we can do to get away from the ho-hum. From Gooey Country Ribs (page 98) to Baseball Park Steak (page 108) and one of my all-time favorites, Salted Eye of the Round Barbecue (page 109)—the meat lovers in your gang will sure be happy.

Yes, a lot of us are eating lighter these days, but that doesn't mean that we can't enjoy our fish and our vegetables with rich barbecued flavor. I promise you'll be surprised by what I've got in my **Sizzling Seafood** and **From Garden to Grill** chapters. Look out for Sweet and Spicy Shrimp (page 113), Steamers on the Grill (page 121), and the great New Orleans taste in Gumbo on the Grill (yes, gumbo made right on the grill—see page 115). And since you've got your grill going anyway, it just makes sense to put all your side dishes on at the same time. Sure, accent your meals with Home-Style Roasted Peppers (page 136), Maple-Grilled Sweet Potatoes (page 130), and Husky Grilled Corn (page 142).

For a big finish, oh, what **Sweet Endings** I've got for your grilled meals! How do these sound for satisfying your sweet tooth:

Chocolate-Stuffed Bananas (page 145), Tutti-frutti Shortcake (page 150), and Waffle Sundaes (page 151)? They sure are fun ways to top off any barbecue!

So, the next time you're looking for a meal in a "snap", look to your barbecue grill and remember: You don't have to wait till the weekend to have fun, quick meals. From tailgate parties and picnics to simple dinners, breakfasts, and lunches at home, use your grill as an extension of your kitchen . . . and bring me along to be your barbecue helper. We'll keep it our secret 'cause, after all, I love it when all your guests say **"OOH it's so GOOD!!**™**"**

Grilling Tips and Information

Choosing a Grill

So, you want to buy a grill. It sounds like an easy thing to do, but there are so many varieties, brands, shapes, sizes, and features to choose from. It sure can be overwhelming! But it doesn't have to be. Here are some tips to help you decide what to look for:

- Think about how you'll want to use your grill—for small or large meals, indoors or outdoors (yup, there are grills that you can use indoors . . . more about those later), at home or to take along on picnics, and fueled by charcoal, gas, or electricity.
- Know your budget. There sure are some reasonably priced grills available as well as some pricier ones. But whatever your price range, know the features you want and find out about the features of the grill you choose. That way you'll get what you want and feel good about your choice.
- What extra features are you looking for? Should your grill be portable? Do you want one with a cover? How about an extra grill rack on top, or a side burner?

xix

Types of Grills

Here's some information that should help you decide which type of grill will best suit your needs.

Charcoal Grills

There are a few different types:

- Most **hibachis** are made of cast iron and are portable but sometimes heavy. They come in a variety of sizes, from tiny ones (perfect for heating snacks and appetizers) to medium-sized ones (good for barbecuing up to a few steaks) and large ones (big enough for preparing complete dinners for 4 to 6).
- **Braziers** are light and portable and are available in different shapes, from barrel to round to square. Smaller ones are often mounted on folding legs, while larger ones usually have wheels attached to their legs (for mobility). Some have adjustable grill racks that can be raised and lowered to change the distance between the charcoal and the cooking surface.
- **Covered kettles** or grills are kettle-shaped and larger than the previous types, with dome-shaped covers that help concentrate the heat in the cooking area, so food cooks more quickly.

Gas Grills

They're usually available only in large sizes, although a few companies make smaller, portable units. Some have permanent briquettes made of lava rocks that heat up again with each use, while others have steel rods or plates that deflect heat. With

gas grills, the grilling heat is easily adjusted by using a knob that controls the flow of gas, similar to a gas range. So, if monitored, gas grills can be very economical since you're using gas only when you need it. Many newer models even have two or three separate control knobs so that you can grill at different temperatures on different areas of the grill at the same time. Side burners and trays, wind screens, covers, and even rotisserie are available on different models. The manufacturers are really giving us some great options!

Electric Grills

A fairly new product, the electric grill is becoming more and more popular because it's so convenient. There are even smokeless models available that can be used inside with proper ventilation. Since electric grills usually don't get as hot as typical gas or charcoal ones, I recommend adding a few minutes to your cooking times. **As with all grills, check your manufacturer's instructions before using**. Consider the differences between gas, charcoal, and electric grills when making your selection:

Gas Grills	Charcoal Grills	Electric Grills
Preheat in minutes	Preheat in 25 to 30 minutes	Preheat in minutes
Easy to regulate heat	Give food an unmistakable flame-broiled flavor	Easy to regulate heat
Quick cleanup	Usually portable and affordable	Portable

Lighting a Barbecue

People always ask me, "What's the best way to light my barbecue?" Well, with a gas grill, it's done 1-2-3. Whether using propane or natural gas, you just open the cover (if there is one), open the gas valve to the igniting position, light it with the starter button or a long match, then set the grill knobs to the desired heat level. **(Follow the manufacturer's directions for starting your particular grill.)** Allow the grill to preheat for 5 to 8 minutes before putting on your food.

Charcoal fires need to preheat for 25 to 40 minutes (depending on how they're started and what temperature you need them at), and lighting them seems to be more of an art. There are so many barbecuing products to choose from, plus everybody's got different ideas about how to do it. **Before starting a charcoal fire, always read and follow the directions on all products being used.** Here are some suggestions for starting a charcoal fire.

- Remove the grill rack. Then, if you like, line the grill with heavy-duty aluminum foil. This makes for easy cleanup! Add **charcoal.** You can buy it either as lumps or briquettes. Lump charcoal will light quicker, but briquettes will burn longer and make a hotter fire. There's even quick-lighting charcoal that has lighter fluid right in it, and charcoal that's packaged in ready-to-light containers. Wow, that sure makes it easy! How much do you need? Enough for a single layer of charcoal under your cooking area. It should actually be spread out just enough to extend 1 to 2 inches beyond the cooking surface being used. (Oh, yes—there are also flavored, smoked wood chips that add a variety of rich flavors. Check them out!)

Charcoal Starters

- **Charcoal lighter** or **starter fluid** is designed to help ignite charcoal. Available in both liquid and jelly forms, it is very flammable. Squirt some (2 to 3 ounces for the average barbecue) lightly onto the **cold** charcoal and let it sit for several minutes. Then ignite with a long wooden match. **Keep the container a safe distance from the grill and** NEVER **add it to lighted or hot coals. Never use any other type of flammable material or gasoline to light barbecue fires. After using lighter fluid to start a barbecue, allow at least 20 minutes before placing any food on the grill, so that the fluid has time to burn off.**
- **Electric starters** are an alternate to lighter fluid. They're long-handled heating elements that are placed on top of charcoal for 10 to 15 minutes until the coals ignite. Once the coals are lit and begin to turn gray, the starter is **carefully** removed. It will be very hot and should be placed on a nonflammable, heat-resistant surface, safely out of anyone's reach.
- **Charcoal chimney starters** are a no-fail way to start your barbecue . . . without lighter fluid or an electric starter! They're round metal canisters that help contain a fire to a small area of the grill until the coals get hot. A chimney starter is placed in the center of a cold barbecue grill, with crumpled newspaper added to the bottom. Then cold charcoal is placed over the newspaper, which is then lit. After the fire burns in the chimney for 20 to 30 minutes, heat/fire-resistant kitchen mitts should be used to remove the chimney. The burning coals are then arranged in a single layer over the bottom of the grill with a long-handled barbecue fork or tongs. The grill rack is then carefully replaced and the fire is ready for cooking.

How Do You Know When the Fire Is Ready for Cooking?

The coals in a charcoal fire are ready when they are glowing and lightly covered with a gray ash. In a charcoal fire, it's the glowing coals that give off the most heat. When the coals are glowing, with gray ash around the edges only, the fire is hot. When the coals are covered with gray ash, the fire isn't as hot because the ash acts as an insulator, keeping the temperature of the coals down.

Some charcoal grills have temperature indicators. If yours doesn't, you can check the temperature simply by placing an oven thermometer (**not** *a meat thermometer*) that goes up to 500°F. on the grill rack and closing the cover. Check the temperature within 5 minutes. Here's a guide for determining the heat of any barbecue fire:

Approximate Temperature	Heat Level
450°F. to 500°F.	Hot
400°F. to 450°F.	Medium-hot
350°F. to 400°F.	Medium
300°F. to 350°F.	Low

If your charcoal fire gets too hot, spread out the coals until they cool down to the desired temperature. Or, if you feel that your fire is too hot or not hot enough for your desired cooking temperature, carefully raise or lower the grill rack over the hot

coals to regulate the temperature. The higher the rack, the lower the temperature. With gas and electric grills, all you have to do is adjust the temperature knob and wait until the temperature adjusts itself.

Grilling Tools
Long-Handled Tools

These are a must because the long handles keep your hands a safe distance from the fire and heat. **Tongs, forks, spatulas,** and **knives** are the indispensable basics that help you turn or flip grilling foods. I think tongs are the most useful because they're like an extra pair of hands, and if you're using charcoal, you can use the tongs to move the coals around. (If you do, just make sure to clean them off before touching food, or have an extra pair on hand just for distributing charcoal.) A **long-handled food brush** is the answer for basting foods with sauces during grilling. It helps if your grill has hooks on it so these tools can be hung close by for easy grabbing!

Hinged Grill Baskets

Boy, are they super! They're two long-handled wire baskets that are hinged together on the top. (They look kind of like two square tennis racquets attached at the top!) Perfect for grilling fish fillets, vegetables, or even steaks because the basket can be flipped over as easily as 1-2-3. And the food holds firmly together inside the basket!

Fire Extinguisher

I think it's a good idea to have a fire extinguisher on hand just in case a fire ever gets out of control. A **small spray bottle of water** usually helps reduce the flames of smaller flare-ups.

Meat Thermometer

Want to know if your steak or chicken is done to the right temperature? Well, here's how: When you think the food is almost done, simply insert the probe of an instant-read thermometer into the thickest part of the meat (not near the bones or into the fat and not so far in that it comes out the other side). Read the temperature. Charts on how to test for doneness for each type of food are at the front of each chapter. This is the best way to tell just how cooked your foods are.

Skewers

Bamboo and metal barbecue skewers range from 6 inches to 12 inches in length. Most of my recipes calling for skewers are meant for 6-inch skewers, but you can use whatever length you prefer and adjust the recipe accordingly. Always soak bamboo skewers in water for 10 to 15 minutes before adding food to be grilled. This will help keep them from burning when placed on the grill. Use tongs or heat/fire-resistant kitchen mitts for removing metal skewers from the grill, and be careful because they get very hot!

Kitchen Mitts

These are very important for grilling and should always be used to prevent burns. The best choice is a heat/fire-resistant type that goes partway up your arm. Never use towels or small pot holders when grilling because they're dangerous and won't do the job.

Aluminum Pans and Foil

These are a great addition to your grilling lineup because they allow you to cook items on the grill that you normally wouldn't consider like Gumbo on the Grill (page 115) and Wrapped-up Cornish Hens (page 60). Make sure to use heavy-duty aluminum foil for grilling, or use two layers of a lighter weight foil.

Wire Grill Brush

This is a stiff metal brush that makes cleanup a breeze! And some grill brushes even have a **grill rack cleaner** attached; those are helpful when you have stubborn, grilled-on food.

Grilling Safety

Remember: Be sure to read the manufacturer's instructions carefully and completely before using any barbecue grill or other grilling or cooking product.

Grilling is a great way to make food in a snap while still having fun. But in order to keep it safe, follow a few basic rules:

1. Make sure the grill is put together correctly, with firmly attached legs and no loose screws or other parts. You don't want it to be unbalanced. That also means placing it on solid, level ground!

2. Never grill inside your home, garage, or anywhere else indoors unless you have a smokeless electric grill that has been approved for indoor use by the grill manufacturer. Outdoors, it's a good idea to keep your barbecue grill at least 10 feet from your house, away from dry grass and leaves. **Whatever type of grill you have, please follow the manufacturer's instructions and use it only in well-ventilated areas.**

3. Never wear loose-fitting clothing that could catch on fire. When grilling, it's a good idea to wear a heavy apron to protect you from grease splatters. Also, as I said before, wear heat/fire-resistant kitchen mitts.

4. After using lighter fluid to start a barbecue, allow at least 20 minutes before placing any food on the grill, so that the fluid has time to burn off. **Never add lighter fluid, gasoline, or other flammables once charcoal is lit**, and **never add any of those to a fire**, even if the coals seem to have gone out! Also, never add those materials or charcoal to a gas grill.

5. If you need to add charcoal to a lit fire, always add it carefully to the area outside the heated coals.

6. Never leave a lit barbecue grill unattended.

7. Unless otherwise instructed, all of the recipes in this book should be made on an uncovered grill. Some flare-ups and flames are expected when grilling, and they usually produce great flavor. But if a flare-up should get larger than you want, remove the food immediately and close the grill cover (if there is one) or carefully spray a charcoal fire lightly with water from a spray bottle until the flames are reduced. If at any time the flames get beyond your control, use common sense and take appropriate actions.

8. Never allow children close to a lit barbecue grill without adult supervision.

Food Safety

Not only do we have safety tips for the grill, but also for the foods that we grill.

1. Don't allow any food to sit in the sun. Food must stay cooled in the refrigerator or in a cold ice chest until ready for grilling or serving.

2. Never put cooked meat, chicken, or fish on the same platter that was used for raw foods unless the platter was washed between uses.

3. Always discard marinades or sauces that have come in contact with raw foods. After marinating or basting with them, they should not be used on cooked foods unless boiled to kill any bacteria that may exist.

4. Don't allow cooked food to sit on the grill after the grill has been turned off or the fire has died out. Cover and refrigerate the cooked food for later use.

xxix

Sauces and Marinades

Instead of a separate chapter on sauces and marinades, I've teamed up some great ones with the chicken, meat, and seafood recipes that I've included in this book. Feel free to mix and match them from one recipe to another to get some new taste combinations. A general rule with sweeter, thicker sauces is to brush them on food toward the end of the grilling. (This prevents burning.) Here are a couple of great all-around barbecue sauces:

My Own Barbecue Sauce

about 1⅓ cups

1 cup ketchup
¼ cup firmly packed brown sugar
2 tablespoons white vinegar
1 tablespoon instant minced onion
2 tablespoons Worcestershire or steak sauce
1 teaspoon dry or 2 tablespoons prepared mustard

In a medium-sized bowl, mix together all the ingredients. Cover and store in the refrigerator until ready to use. Stir again before brushing on chicken or beef near the end of its cooking time.

Country Sweet and Sour Sauce

about 3 cups

1 bottle (12 ounces) chili sauce
1¼ cups grape jelly
2 teaspoons dry mustard

In a medium-sized saucepan, mix together all the ingredients. Heat over low heat for 5 to 8 minutes, or until the jelly melts and the mixture is well combined. Use immediately for brushing on chicken, beef, or fish near the end of its cooking time, or cool slightly and transfer to a medium-sized bowl, cover, and store in the refrigerator until ready to use.

How Do You Know When It's Done?

Just the way cooking and baking times vary slightly from one oven to another, cooking times may vary from one grill to another, also. All equipment is different, and all grill calibration is not exact. Also, most grills have areas that are hotter than others. Learn the hot spots on your grill and work around them by rotating the food, or use the hot spots for the items that are to be well done. When you are grilling outdoors, there are additional factors that affect cooking time, such as air temperature, humidity, and wind. Be aware of these when planning your grilling times and adjust accordingly. Use the times given in the recipes as guides

and test for doneness after the minimum suggested times. (You can always give it a bit longer.) When burgers, chicken, steak, and fish are almost done, make a small slit in the center to see if they're cooked to your liking. See the tips at the front of each chapter for more specifics on testing each type of food for doneness.

Grilled Hamburger, Hot Dog, and Sausage Toppers

As I travel around the country, I get to see all the different types of foods eaten in different areas, as well as different ways people serve the same dishes. For example, I've put together a list of toppings—from traditional to unusual—that I've tried myself or seen others use on their hamburgers, hot dogs, and sausage. Give them a try alone or in different combinations! (I've left a few lines at the end of my list for you to add your own discoveries.)

Mustard There are lots of types and flavors, from yellow to horseradish to deli-style to spicy brown.

Ketchup Ketchup isn't just plain ketchup anymore! There are some great spiced ketchups available now.

Relish There are lots of types, from sweet to tangy.

Barbecue sauce There are lots of easy recipes for making barbecue sauce, but it's even easier to buy a prepared one—and there are loads of brands and flavors available, from smoky to honey- and fruit-flavored ones.

Chopped onions Try sweet, red, or white.

Sautéed vegetables Start with sliced or chopped mushrooms, onions, and bell peppers alone or combined. Then maybe try zucchini, eggplant, and others.

Salsa This is such a popular flavoring, and you can choose from smooth to chunky and mild to hot.

Chili Homemade or canned, it's a hearty addition.

Hot pepper sauce Red or green, it adds a real zip!

Dressings Use your favorites, but Russian and ranch are especially good on grilled foods.

Cheese Add your favorites, but cheeses that melt easily, like Cheddar and Monterey Jack, work best. You can even buy them already shredded or sliced.

Sauerkraut Served hot or cold, it's an old-time hot dog favorite.

Sliced jalapeño peppers Fresh or processed, these can be shockingly hot, so always ask your eaters before adding them!!

Cooked bacon in strips or crumbled, or bacon bits For that popular smoky flavor.

Shredded lettuce and chopped tomatoes Add a garden fresh flavor to all your grilled items.

Cleanup

After cooking a quick meal on the barbecue, you'll want to be able to clean up your grill in a snap so it'll be ready for the next time—with little work. Preparing and cleaning up with little work . . . now *that's* my type of cooking! Here are a few tricks to keep cleanup a breeze:

1. If using a gas grill, leave the grill on high for 8 to 10 minutes after removing the cooked food. Turn off the gas and wait for the fire to die out. On a charcoal grill, lower the grill rack as low as possible to burn off remaining food particles.
2. For all types of grills, use a grill brush to clean the rack(s). You can also remove grill racks once they've cooled and hose down the racks. Wipe down the rest of the grill with hot soapy water.
3. You can safely dump the charcoal after the coals have completely burned out and have cooled. Then wipe out the fire bowl so it's ready to use the next time.
4. It's also a good idea to check on the amount of propane or charcoal you have left so that you are prepared for your next barbecue.

Grill Storage

1. Empty the drip tray underneath the grill after each use to prevent a buildup of grease and a potential fire hazard.
2. Put the grill away only after the fire has been extinguished and the grill has been completely cooled and cleaned.
3. Store your grill indoors if possible, or outdoors if covered.
4. Do not store propane inside.

Notes from MR. FOOD®

Top It . . . or Not?

There are some recipes in here that call for closing the grill cover. Although most grills manufactured today have grill covers, some don't. If yours doesn't, you can still make these recipes. Just cover the foods with aluminum foil and adjust your cooking times, always being sure to cook foods until done.

Lighten Up . . . with Cooking Sprays

Throughout this book and in my other cookbooks I frequently mention nonstick vegetable cooking spray and recommend using it to coat cookware and bakeware before placing food in or on them. Here's why—these sprays are easy to use, they add no measurable amount of fat to our food, and now they're even available in nonaerosol *and* in flavored varieties! The flavored sprays are super ways to add a touch of taste, either before or after cooking foods, without adding fat and calories. **But remember: Spray only *cold* cookware or grill racks with the sprays. They should never be sprayed into or near open flames or heat sources.** So far I've tried butter, olive oil, garlic, mesquite, Italian, and Oriental flavors. I think they do a great job of "greasing" *without* the grease.

Serving Sizes

I like to serve generous-sized portions myself, so I generally figure that way when I list the number of portions to expect from my recipes. That way you can have a good idea of how many people you can expect to serve with each dish. Yes, appetites do vary and *you* know the special food loves of your eaters, so, as always, you be the judge of how much to make.

Packaged Foods

Packaged food sizes may vary by brand. Generally, the sizes indicated in these recipes are average sizes. If you can't find the exact package size listed in the ingredients, whatever package is closest in size will usually do the trick.

Munchies on the Grill

Move over potato chips and dip, 'cause here come some fun, easy, quick munchies that you can create right on your grill. Boy, oh boy, what a great way to start your outdoor get-togethers and help those rumbling tummies. Here are some grilled munchie suggestions:

1. Have munchies ready as your guests arrive. It's a nice way to keep the gang happy until the hearty grilling begins!
2. Make a double batch of any of these, since everybody's usually hungry when they first get to a barbecue.
3. Why not make a meal of just munchies? When a bunch of treats are made on the grill, you've got an anytime snack or a complete meal!

Munchies on the Grill

Grilled Fajita Roll-ups

16 pieces

When I go out, I love to make a meal of just appetizers! If you do, too, then why not make a bunch of appetizers on the grill? Fajitas are full of the stuff everybody loves, so make 'em a snack or make 'em a meal!

8 8-inch flour tortillas
8 thin slices (about ½ pound) deli-style roast beef
8 thin tomato slices
8 very thin onion slices
½ cup (2 ounces) shredded Cheddar cheese, divided
Salsa for dipping

Preheat the grill to medium heat. In the center of each tortilla, layer one slice each of the roast beef, tomato, and onion and about 1 tablespoon of cheese. Roll up each tortilla, tucking in the sides while rolling. Place in a disposable 9" × 13" aluminum baking pan. Place the pan on the grill and cover with aluminum foil; cook for 8 to 10 minutes, turning the tortillas occasionally until they are heated through, the cheese is melted, and the outsides are lightly browned. Cut in half crosswise and serve with salsa for dipping.

NOTE: Bring out the Tex-Mex taste even more by adding a few sliced jalapeño peppers to each roll-up. Wow!

Toasted Garlic Slices

6 to 8 servings

They're appetizers—no, no, they're dinner "go-alongs"... Well, it doesn't matter what you call them, 'cause they're ready to eat in just minutes, and the grill gives them a nice smoky taste that'll keep the gang coming back for more!

½ cup (1 stick) butter or margarine, melted
1 teaspoon garlic powder
1 teaspoon salt
1 loaf (1 pound) French or Italian bread, cut in half lengthwise

Preheat the grill to medium heat. Place the melted butter in a small bowl. Stir in the garlic powder and salt. Brush the mixture over the cut sides of the bread. With the grill cover closed, grill the bread, cut sides down, for 5 to 7 minutes, or until the bread is crispy and golden. Remove the bread from the heat and cut diagonally into 1-inch slices. Serve immediately.

NOTE: Why not cut the bread into larger slices and use them instead of buns for your favorite hamburgers? Yummy!

Hearty Mushrooms

6 servings

Who doesn't like the taste of steak and mushrooms? Well, here's a great meal starter that combines those two great tastes in one easy recipe . . . and you can serve it right from the grill!

½ cup bottled steak sauce
1 clove garlic, chopped
2 tablespoons vegetable oil
1 pound fresh mushrooms, lightly rinsed and dried

Preheat the grill to medium-high heat. In a medium-sized bowl, combine all the ingredients and stir until the mushrooms are evenly coated. Pour into a 9" × 13" disposable aluminum pan and grill for 5 to 7 minutes, tossing occasionally until the mixture is hot and the mushrooms are tender.

NOTE: Serve these with toothpicks, but be sure to let the mushrooms cool a bit first. (The insides stay very hot for a while!) These are also gangbusters served over Bourbon Steak (page 99).

Dip at the Grill

4 cups

You can make and serve this party dip indoors, but when you do it on your barbecue grill, the person doing the grilling will finally have some company!

1 pound Italian or your favorite sausage, casings removed
1 tablespoon dried oregano
1 cup (4 ounces) shredded Cheddar cheese
1 clove garlic, minced
1 jar (15½ to 16 ounces) ready-made chili recipe
1 package (8 ounces) cream cheese, broken up

Preheat the grill to medium heat. On the grill, crumble and brown the sausage in a large cast-iron or other heat-resistant skillet. Drain the fat, then add the remaining ingredients. On a gas or electric grill, reduce the heat to low. On a charcoal grill, raise the rack to about 6 inches from the heat. Simmer the mixture until it thickens and the cheese is melted, about 5 minutes. Immediately place the pan on the edge of the grill to keep it warm and use right from the grill as a dip for crackers or pieces of crunchy bread.

NOTE: Try serving this with Pita Crisps (page 7).

Pita Crisps

64 to 80 wedges

If you ever had these tasty pita crisps and thought they'd be tough to make, boy, were you wrong! They're easy, quick, and yes, can be cooked right on your grill.

1½ cups (3 sticks) butter, melted
3 packages (1.15 ounces each) onion soup mix
8 to 10 medium-sized (5 to 6 inches) pitas,
sliced into 8 wedges each

Preheat the grill to medium-high heat. In a small bowl, combine the melted butter and soup mix; mix well. Place the pita wedges in a large bowl and toss with half of the butter mixture, coating well. Pour the remaining butter mixture into the bowl and toss again. Grill the pita wedges for 2 to 3 minutes per side, until brown and crispy.

NOTE: Serve these crisp, oniony wedges as a "go-along" for hamburgers or hot dogs, instead of potato chips. They're also great with Dip at the Grill (page 6) and Hot Seafood Spread (page 13). And the best part is, they can be stored in an airtight container for up to 2 weeks!

Mexican Pita Pizza

6 to 8 servings

More and more pizzerias are making their pizzas in wood-burning ovens. And if you've ever tasted them, you know why wood-fired pizzas have become so popular. Want to get that same smoky taste from your barbecue grill—but at a fraction of the cost? Here's how...

4 large (about 8 inches) pitas
½ cup vegetable oil
1⅓ cups salsa, divided
2 cups (8 ounces) shredded Monterey Jack cheese, divided
1 can (2.25 ounces) sliced black olives, drained, divided
1 can (4 ounces) chopped green chilies, drained, divided

Preheat the grill to medium heat. Brush one side of each pita with the oil. Place the pitas on a disposable aluminum baking pan and top each one with ⅓ cup salsa, ½ cup cheese, 1½ tablespoons olives, and 2 teaspoons chilies. Place the pan on the grill, close the grill cover, and grill the pizzas for 5 minutes, or until the cheese is melted and the crust begins to crisp. Remove from the heat and cut the pizzas into quarters.

NOTE: I usually use medium-hot salsa, but go with a milder or hotter one if you prefer.

8

Cheesy Burger Bites

24 "bites"

Why not tame the appetite of everybody in your gang with this guaranteed winner? They're mini-hamburgers smothered with cheese ... and since they're fun and tasty, maybe you should make a double batch.

1½ pounds ground beef
½ teaspoon salt
¼ teaspoon pepper
24 slices cocktail party rye bread
12 dollops any flavor prepared cheese spread

-Preheat the grill to medium-high heat. In a large bowl, combine the ground beef, salt, and pepper. Using a small ice cream scoop, form the beef mixture into 12 meatballs. Flatten the meatballs to ½-inch thickness and grill for 5 to 6 minutes, turning once. Remove the cooked mini-hamburgers from the grill, place each one on a slice of cocktail party rye bread, and top with a dollop of the cheese spread. (The heat from the burgers will melt the cheese.) Top the mini-hamburgers with the remaining bread slices and cut in half for bite-sized hors d'oeuvres.

NOTE: Cheese spread can be found in the dairy section of the grocery store. There are so many flavors available, why not try a different one each time you make these? That way you can have a new taste treat every time!

Hot Greek-Style Dip

1½ to 2 cups

While you're waiting for all your favorite main dishes to cook on the grill, whether they're burgers, chicken, or steaks, this dip will surely satisfy your "munchies"!

1 package (8 ounces) cream cheese
½ cup (4 ounces) crumbled feta cheese
2 tablespoons chopped fresh parsley
½ teaspoon minced garlic (1 to 2 cloves)
½ teaspoon dried oregano
½ teaspoon dried basil
⅛ teaspoon pepper

Preheat the grill to medium heat. In a food processor or blender, mix all the ingredients until well blended. Place the mixture in a 5" × 8" disposable aluminum pan. Place the pan on the grill and cook, uncovered, for 7 to 9 minutes, stirring often until the dip is heated through and bubbly.

NOTE: This is great served immediately or kept warm on the side of the grill. Try it with Pita Crisps (page 7).

Clams on the Racks

2 dozen

I can't believe how easy these are! I'm almost embarrassed when my family tells me how good they are, since I know that the grill did all the work. (It gives the clams a nutty, rich flavor.)

24 Mahogany, littleneck, or cherrystone clams,
soaked in ice water for 30 minutes

Preheat the grill to high heat. Place the clams on the grill racks (yes, right on the grill racks) and close the grill cover. Cook for 7 to 9 minutes, or until the clams open wide. **Discard any clams that do not open by themselves.**

NOTE: Dip the cooked clams in melted butter, but be careful when picking them up because the liquid from inside the clam shells will be very hot.

Melted Nacho Supremes

6 to 8 servings

No one will be late for the barbecue when they find out what will be on the grill for starters ... no one!!

1 package (9 ounces) tortilla chips
1 can (2.25 ounces) sliced black olives, drained
1 can (4 ounces) sliced jalapeño peppers, drained
1½ cups (6 ounces) shredded Cheddar cheese

Preheat the grill to medium heat. Place the tortilla chips in a 9" × 13" disposable aluminum pan. Sprinkle the chips with the olives, jalapeños, and cheese, then cover with aluminum foil. Use a knife to make several small slits in the aluminum foil cover to allow steam to escape while cooking. Grill for 6 to 8 minutes, or until the cheese is melted.

NOTE: These are super as is, or you might want to serve them topped with sour cream, guacamole, or salsa.

Hot Seafood Spread

8 to 10 servings

How could two ingredients and little work be so lip-smacking good?! If you serve this as your appetizer, everybody'll be so anxious to see what you've got planned for dinner!

2 packages (8 ounces each) cream cheese, softened
2 cups (12 ounces) shredded crabmeat or imitation crabmeat

Preheat the grill to medium heat. In a medium-sized bowl, combine the cream cheese and crabmeat with an electric beater until thoroughly mixed. Pour into an 8-inch square disposable aluminum pan, and grill for 10 minutes, stirring occasionally.

NOTE: Serve with crackers, Pita Crisps (page 7), or cocktail party rye bread. Just dip 'em or spread 'em and watch it disappear!

Magical Salami Cups

18 to 20 slices

I'm not sure if these are more fun to eat or make because they curl into cups right before your eyes . . . like magic!

1 pound salami, sliced ⅓ inch thick
½ cup duck sauce or sweet-and-sour sauce
¼ teaspoon hot pepper sauce

Preheat the grill to medium heat. Grill the salami slices for 3 to 4 minutes, until they curl into the shape of shallow cups. Do not turn the slices. In a small bowl, combine the sauces. Fill each salami cup with about 1 teaspoon of the sauce and serve.

NOTE: This is great as an hors d'oeuvre or for just plain old snacking!

Hot 'n' Spicy Nut Snacks

3 cups

You know that song about "chestnuts roasting on an open fire"? Well, now that we can cook our nuts on the barbecue, I bet somebody'll write a new version!

3 cups whole unsalted nuts (like almonds, walnuts, and pecans)
2 tablespoons vegetable oil
¼ teaspoon cayenne pepper
½ cup granulated sugar
2 tablespoons brown sugar

Preheat the grill to medium heat. In a medium-sized bowl, combine the nuts with the oil until well coated. In a small bowl, combine the remaining ingredients. Place the nuts in a colander placed over a bowl. Pour the sugar mixture over the nuts and shake the colander to coat the nuts and allow any excess sugar mixture to fall into the bowl below. If the nuts are not completely coated, pour the excess sugar mixture over them and shake again. Place the coated nuts in an 8-inch square disposable aluminum pan. Grill in the pan for 6 to 8 minutes, mixing frequently to keep them from burning. Let the nuts cool slightly before serving.

NOTE: Why not make this with a 16-ounce can of assorted unsalted nuts? That way, you can get a selection of nuts in every bite.

Spinach Pizza

6 to 8 slices

They'll never believe it, so make sure you have a helper to witness that this **"OOH it's so GOOD!!™"** came right off the grill!

1 (12- or 14-inch) ready-made pizza crust
½ teaspoon vegetable oil
1 tablespoon Italian seasoning
¼ cup grated Parmesan cheese
1 package (10 ounces) frozen chopped spinach,
thawed and drained well
1 cup (4 ounces) shredded mozzarella cheese

Wrap a 12- or 14-inch pizza pan in aluminum foil. Place the pizza crust on the foil-covered pan and rub oil on top of the crust. Sprinkle with the Italian seasoning and Parmesan cheese. In a small bowl, combine the spinach and mozzarella cheese, then sprinkle evenly over the pizza crust. Place the pan on the grill and close the cover. Grill the pizza for 10 to 12 minutes, or until the cheese is melted and the crust begins to crisp.

NOTE: Add other pizza toppings if you want, like black olives, onion slices, and chopped tomatoes. And for a fresh garden taste, try using 2 cups of chopped fresh spinach instead of frozen.

Ground Beef Fajitas

4 servings

I like making these as a before-meal snack. You know those times when you wait and wait for everybody to show up? With these on the grill, you won't mind the wait!

1 pound lean ground beef
1 large onion, cut into thin wedges
1 green or red bell pepper, cored, cleaned, and cut lengthwise
into thin strips
1 cup mild salsa
2 teaspoons chili powder
8 8-inch flour tortillas

Preheat the grill to medium-high heat. On the grill, brown the ground beef, onion, and pepper in a large cast iron or other heat-resistant skillet for 8 to 10 minutes, or until the beef is no longer pink, stirring occasionally. Pour off the drippings. Stir in the salsa and chili powder. Reduce the heat to low or raise the grill rack. Cook for 5 more minutes, stirring occasionally. Roll the beef mixture in the tortillas and serve immediately.

NOTE: My favorite way to serve these is with a choice of toppings—anything from chopped tomatoes and onions to sour cream, shredded Cheddar cheese, and more salsa. There are no rules, so make them your own!

17

Honey-Mustard Bologna

6 to 8 servings

Sometimes the simple treats are the best, and with this easy, toss-on-the-grill munchie, you'll see why...

2 teaspoons honey
3 tablespoons prepared mustard
1 whole (12-ounce) bologna, unsliced

Heat the grill to medium-high. In a small bowl, combine the honey and mustard. Set aside half of the mixture in a bowl for dipping, and coat the bologna with the other half. Double-wrap and tightly seal the bologna in aluminum foil. Grill for 18 to 20 minutes, or until the center is heated through and the glaze begins to caramelize. Unwrap the bologna and cut into 1-inch pieces. Serve with the reserved honey-mustard dipping sauce.

NOTE: A whole 12-ounce bologna should be available in or near the deli department of your supermarket.

Raspberry Brie

5 to 6 servings

Here's a sure way to be the talk of the barbecue . . . and you can make this in just 5 minutes!

1 wheel (4.5 ounces) Brie or Camembert
1 tablespoon raspberry jam or preserves

Preheat the grill to medium heat. Place the wheel of cheese on the grill for 5 to 6 minutes, turning it over halfway through the grilling. Spoon the preserves over the cheese and let them warm for another minute.

NOTE: Serve this immediately with Pita Crisps (page 7), plain bagel chips, or crackers. **And don't leave the cheese on the grill any longer than 6 minutes because it'll get too soft and messy!**

Beyond Basic Burgers

What's more traditional than hamburgers on the grill? And with these helpful hints, you'll be ready to hit the grill like a pro:

1. I usually use an 80/20 ground beef mixture. That means that the meat is 80% lean meat and 20% fat. I think this blend makes burgers with the best taste and texture, but you can buy leaner beef with less fat, if you prefer.
2. Make all your burgers the same size and shape so that they cook at the same rate.
3. Burgers will shrink during cooking, so I suggest making them larger than you would like them to end up. (Then, after they shrink, you end up with just the right size burger.) Most of these recipes call for 1 to 1¼ pounds of ground beef. For that amount, I recommend making 4 burgers that are about ¾ inch thick and 4 inches wide. That way they should be thick and juicy.
4. Don't press down on the burgers with a spatula (or any other implement) while the burgers are cooking. This squeezes out the juices! We want our burgers to keep their moistness and flavor.
5. To toast a hamburger bun, place the cut side down on the grill for 1 to 2 minutes, just before the burgers will be done.
6. There are so many possibilities for topping burgers! Check out the list on pages xxxii–xxxiii and try different toppings every time.

Beyond Basic Burgers

Salsa Burgers

4 burgers

Since salsa is America's favorite condiment, this recipe should be a sure winner at your house. And, of course, you can really spice it up with hot salsa for an extra loud "Olé!"

1 to 1¼ pounds ground beef
½ cup medium salsa
¼ cup dry bread crumbs

Preheat the grill to medium-high heat. In a medium-sized bowl, combine all the ingredients; mix well. Divide the mixture into 4 equal amounts and make 4 patties. Grill them for 8 to 12 minutes, or until desired doneness, turning them over halfway through the grilling.

NOTE: Why not top each burger with a teaspoon of guacamole for a Tex-Mex flair? Have fun with these!

Bacon Burgers

4 burgers

Move over, fast-food burgers! We can make these homemade bacon burgers on our grills in no time. And since the bacon is mixed right into the ground beef, we get great flavor through and through!

1 to 1¼ pounds ground beef
¼ cup (10 slices) crisply cooked, chopped bacon
2 tablespoons dry bread crumbs

Preheat the grill to medium-high heat. In a medium-sized bowl, combine all the ingredients; mix well. Divide the mixture into 4 equal amounts and make 4 patties. Grill them for 8 to 12 minutes, or until desired doneness, turning them over halfway through the grilling.

NOTE: If you don't want to use real bacon, of course you can use dried bottled bacon bits. A quarter of a cup will do the trick.

Cheesy Herbed Patties

4 patties

If you think that cream cheese belongs only on bagels, think again! With the addition of herb cream cheese to these turkey patties, you'll be sure to raise some eyebrows around the picnic table.

1 to 1¼ pounds ground turkey
2 tablespoons herb cream cheese
2 tablespoons Italian style dry bread crumbs
1½ teaspoons salt
½ teaspoon pepper

Preheat the grill to medium-high heat. In a medium-sized bowl, combine all the ingredients; mix well. Divide the mixture into 4 equal amounts and make 4 patties. Grill them for 8 to 12 minutes, until no pink remains and the patties are cooked through completely, turning them over halfway through the grilling.

NOTE: Herb cream cheese is available in the refrigerator section of the supermarket, near the other specialty cream cheeses.

Good Ol' American Hamburgers

4 burgers

Sometimes there's nothing better than a "good ol' American hamburger." In this case, simple is best!

1 to 1¼ pounds ground beef
¼ teaspoon onion powder
1½ teaspoons salt
1 teaspoon pepper
4 hamburger buns

Preheat the grill to medium-high heat. In a medium-sized bowl, combine all the ingredients except the hamburger buns; mix well. Divide the mixture into 4 equal amounts and make 4 patties. Grill them for 8 to 12 minutes, or until desired doneness, turning them over halfway through the grilling. Serve on buns.

NOTE: For a list of my favorite toppings, see pages xxxii–xxxiii. I prefer ground meat with an 80/20 blend, which means 80% lean beef and 20% fat ground in. Yes, fat, because the fat adds moisture and flavor.

Jalapeño Cheese Burgers

4 burgers

Here's an easy way to add some kick to your burgers 'cause the jalapeños are already in the cheese!

1 to 1¼ pounds ground beef
½ cup (2 ounces) shredded Monterey Jack or Cheddar cheese
with jalapeños
2 tablespoons dry bread crumbs
½ teaspoon salt
¼ teaspoon pepper

Preheat the grill to medium-high heat. In a medium-sized bowl, combine all the ingredients; mix well. Divide the mixture into 4 equal amounts and make 4 patties. Grill them for 8 to 12 minutes, or until desired doneness, turning them over halfway through the grilling.

NOTE: If you prefer, you can use ½ cup Swiss or plain Cheddar cheese for a creamy cheeseburger without the jalapeño bite.

27

Peppered Turkey Burgers

4 burgers

The next time you go grocery shopping, why not pick up some ground turkey? The trick to cooking with it is to season it heavily ... The results are yummy and you can bet they'll "gobble" it up at home.

1 to 1¼ pounds ground turkey
1 tablespoon dry red wine
1½ teaspoons salt
4 teaspoons pepper

Preheat the grill to medium-high heat. In a medium-sized bowl, combine all the ingredients; mix well. Divide the mixture into 4 equal amounts and make 4 patties. Grill them for 8 to 12 minutes, or until no pink remains and the burgers are cooked completely through, turning them over halfway through the grilling.

NOTE: Serve these on toasted hard rolls or hamburger buns. Try adding a slice of tomato and a dollop of mayonnaise to each one, too.

Ranch Burgers

4 burgers

The secret in these burgers is the combination of ranch dressing and tortilla chips—the dressing gives them the flavor . . . the chips give them the texture . . . and you'll give them a thumbs-up!

1 to 1¼ pounds ground beef
2 tablespoons ranch dressing
¼ cup crushed tortilla chips (see Note)
¼ teaspoon salt
⅛ teaspoon pepper

Preheat the grill to medium-high heat. In a medium-sized bowl, combine all the ingredients; mix well. Divide the mixture into 4 equal amounts and make 4 patties. Grill them for 8 to 12 minutes, or until desired doneness, turning them over halfway through the grilling.

NOTE: The best way to crush the chips is to put them in a plastic bag and roll them with a rolling pin or the side of a heavy food can.

Hamburger "Hot Dogs"

8 "dogs"

It's a hot dog... no, no, it's a burger. But I thought burgers were flat...?! Okay, it's a burger in the shape of a hot dog—with the condiments baked right in!

8 wooden or metal skewers
1 to 1¼ pounds ground beef
2 tablespoons ketchup
2 teaspoons prepared mustard
¼ cup sweet relish
¼ cup dry bread crumbs

If using wooden skewers, soak them in water for 15 to 20 minutes. Preheat the grill to medium-high heat. In a medium-sized bowl, combine the remaining ingredients; mix well. Divide the mixture into 8 equal amounts and shape each one into a "hot dog" about 6 inches long. Insert a skewer through the center of each "hot dog" (like ice cream on a stick). Cover and chill in the refrigerator for about 30 minutes, or in the freezer for up to 10 minutes, to help these keep their shape during grilling. Place the "hot dogs" across the grill rack and grill for 8 to 12 minutes, or until desired doneness, turning after 3 minutes and turning occasionally thereafter.

NOTE: Sure, there's ketchup and mustard already grilled into these, but you can always use more for topping. And check my list of topping suggestions on pages xxxii–xxxiii, too.

30

Veal Patties

4 patties

If your family loves grilled hamburgers but wants a little change from regular beef burgers this season, why not try using ground veal instead? Veal isn't just for fancy dinners anymore!

1 to 1¼ pounds ground veal
1 egg, beaten
¼ cup dry bread crumbs
½ teaspoon salt
¼ teaspoon pepper

Preheat the grill to medium-high heat. In a medium-sized bowl, combine all the ingredients; mix well. Divide the mixture into 4 equal amounts and make 4 patties. Grill them for 8 to 12 minutes, or until desired doneness, turning them over halfway through the grilling.

NOTE: You can usually find ground veal already packaged in the supermarket meat department. Give ground veal a try—it's priced much lower than traditional veal cuts.

Oriental Burgers

4 burgers

East meets West when you combine these tastes of the Orient with the All-American hamburger . . . and the results are out of this world!

1 to 1¼ pounds ground beef
1 tablespoon soy sauce
1 to 2 cloves garlic, minced
1 tablespoon sesame seeds
¼ teaspoon ground ginger
½ cup cold cooked rice

Preheat the grill to medium-high heat. In a medium-sized bowl, combine all the ingredients; mix well. Divide the mixture into 4 equal amounts and make 4 patties. Grill them for 8 to 12 minutes, or until desired doneness, turning them over halfway through the grilling.

NOTE: Don't forget that bottled chopped garlic works just as well as fresh. It's usually available in the supermarket produce department.

32

Taco Burgers

4 burgers

Everybody likes tacos, but how many of us ever made them on the grill?! *"Wow" is just the beginning of this recipe. (Yes, it's correct—there are only three ingredients!)*

1 to 1¼ pounds ground beef
1 package (1.25 ounces) dry taco seasoning mix
4 crusty hard rolls

Preheat the grill to medium-high heat. In a medium-sized bowl, combine the ground beef and the taco mix; mix well. Divide the mixture into 4 equal amounts and make 4 patties. Grill them for 8 to 12 minutes, or until desired doneness, turning them over halfway through the grilling. Serve on the rolls.

NOTE: Taco seasoning mix is available in the supermarket spice section or in the ethnic foods section. If you serve these burgers with bowls of shredded iceberg lettuce, chopped tomatoes, and shredded Monterey Jack cheese, you'll have your own taco burger buffet!

Onion Chili Burgers

8 burgers

This is the perfect every-occasion get-together burger because, after all, the combination of onion and chili flavors is impossible to resist!

2½ pounds ground beef
1 envelope (from a 2.4-ounce box) dry onion soup mix
⅓ cup water
⅓ cup chili sauce
¼ cup finely chopped green bell pepper
¼ teaspoon black pepper

Preheat the grill to medium-high heat. In a medium-sized bowl, combine all the ingredients; mix well. Divide the mixture into 8 equal amounts and make 8 patties. Grill them for 8 to 12 minutes, or until desired doneness, turning them over halfway through the grilling.

NOTE: If you want to plan ahead, you can mix up this full recipe, make half of the patties for tonight's dinner, and freeze the rest of the patties (uncooked) for no longer than 30 days (to keep their full flavor). Just thaw them overnight in the fridge and cook them according to the directions above.

Veal Parmesan Burgers

4 burgers

Imagine the taste of Veal Parmesan from your favorite Italian restaurant, made with the ease of cooking on the grill. With a side dish of spaghetti, you'll be saying, **"OOH sono BUONO!!"**

1 to 1¼ pounds ground veal
¼ cup crushed tomatoes
2 tablespoons grated Parmesan cheese
½ teaspoon garlic powder
½ teaspoon dried oregano
¼ teaspoon salt
¼ teaspoon pepper

Preheat the grill to medium-high heat. In a medium-sized bowl, combine all the ingredients; mix well. Divide the mixture into 4 equal amounts and make 4 patties. Grill them for 8 to 12 minutes, or until desired doneness, turning them over halfway through the grilling.

NOTE: Try serving these on slices of crusty Italian bread. I've even heated a cup of bottled spaghetti sauce in the microwave just before serving to use as a topping. And if you make an antipasto salad to go along with it . . . you've got your own Italian festival!

35

Hot Diggity Dogs and Sausage, Too

We eat them at the ballpark and when we're at tailgate picnics and backyard barbecues. They're great for a quick supper, too, or for an anytime simple snack. Here are a few hot dog tips:

1. Hot dogs come in a variety of sizes, usually between 4 and 8 per pound (The more hot dogs you get per pound, the smaller the hot dogs will be.)
2. Today there are so many types of hot dogs—all-beef, pork, chicken, and turkey. And, of course, you can use any of them in my recipes.
3. When you buy hot dogs, they've already been completely cooked. So when you're preparing them, all you really have to do is heat them. Of course, everybody likes them done their own way, so cook them the way your gang wants—from just warmed to browned to bursting.
4. There are so many sausage selections! You can choose from bulk, links, spicy, and mild breakfast sausage. ANd sausage can be pork, turkey, or even a kosher type made from beef, veal, or turkey.
5. Whenever you cook sausage, be sure that it's thoroughly and completely cooked.
6. Top your hot dogs with all your favorites—and try some new toppings for a change, like the ones on pages xxxii–xxxiii.

Hot Diggity Dogs and Sausage, Too

Shish-Ke-Dog

6 skewers

Here's the answer to fancying up "just a hot dog" into an "ooh-la-la" barbecue treat.

6 wooden or metal skewers
5 to 6 hot dogs, each cut into 3 equal pieces
1 small red or green bell pepper, cut into 1-inch chunks
1 small onion, cut into 1-inch chunks

If using wooden skewers, soak them in water for 15 to 20 minutes. Preheat the grill to medium-high heat. Thread a piece of hot dog, then pepper, and then onion onto each skewer; repeat until all the chunks are used. Grill for 10 to 12 minutes, turning occasionally. Serve with ketchup and mustard, as desired.

NOTE: For a great summer meal, serve these with scoops of potato salad and a garden salad on the side.

Hot Dog "Lasagna"

6 to 8 servings

This isn't your usual noodle type of lasagna, but the layers of sliced hot dogs, beans, and cheese give it a lasagna look. It's great for a potluck barbecue. Just place it on the grill and enjoy!

2 cans (16 onces each) vegetarian baked beans, drained
1 pound hot dogs, sliced into ¼-inch-thick diagonal slices
1½ cups (6 ounces) shredded Monterey Jack cheese

Preheat the grill to medium-high heat. In a disposable 8-inch square aluminum pan, layer half of the beans, then half of the hot dogs, and then half of the cheese. Repeat with remaining beans, hot dogs, and cheese. Cover the pan tightly with aluminum foil and place on the grill. Close the grill cover and heat the beans for 10 to 12 minutes, or until the cheese is completely melted and the hot dogs and beans are heated through.

NOTE: This can be put together ahead of time, then kept covered and refrigerated (uncooked). Cook it when you're ready, but add 4 to 5 minutes to the cooking time.

Cheese Dogs

8 "dogs"

We've all grown up with traditional cheeseburgers. Well, it's time to introduce your family to cheese dogs. And after they taste them, you'll be the top dog!

8 hot dogs
4 slices American cheese, cut into 4 strips each

Preheat the grill to medium-high heat. Slit each hot dog lengthwise about ¼ inch deep. Grill the hot dogs for about 5 minutes, turning them occasionally. Tuck 2 strips of cheese into the slit of each hot dog. Grill again, cheese side up, for another 2 to 4 minutes, or until the cheese is melted.

NOTE: That's all there is to it! Serve on hot dog rolls with your usual hot dog toppings (pages xxxii–xxxiii) and watch these disappear.

Kielbasa on a Skewer

4 to 6 servings

Here's a super "make ahead, throw on the grill" treat that'll excite the whole picnic gang.

1 medium-sized zucchini, cut into about 12 1-inch chunks
1 medium-sized onion, cut into about 12 1-inch chunks
1 large red bell pepper, cored and cut into
about 12 1-inch chunks
1 cup Italian dressing
1 pound kielbasa, cut into about 18 1-inch chunks
6 wooden or metal skewers

Place the vegetable chunks in a medium-sized bowl and add the Italian dressing. Cover and allow the vegetables to marinate in the refrigerator for at least 2 hours or overnight. If using wooden skewers, soak them in water for 15 to 20 minutes. Preheat the grill to medium-high heat. Then thread 1 chunk each of kielbasa, zucchini, onion, and pepper onto each skewer. Repeat, and finish each skewer with a chunk of kielbasa. Grill for 15 to 18 minutes, turning occasionally, until the vegetables are tender-crisp and the kielbasa is heated through.

NOTE: If you want, you can use green or yellow bell pepper chunks instead of red . . . or even some of each!

Greek-Style Hot Dog Sauce

4 cups (enough for 12 to 18 hot dogs)

Wanna hit a home run the next time you serve hot dogs? Here's a topping that could please the whole ballpark... yup, even the umpires!

¼ cup vegetable oil
2 cups finely chopped onion
1½ pounds ground beef
1 teaspoon (3 cloves) chopped garlic
2 tablespoons chili powder
2 tablespoons paprika
1 tablespoon dried oregano
2 teaspoons salt
½ teaspoon pepper

In a large saucepan, heat the oil over medium-high heat on the stove top and sauté the onions until golden. Add the ground beef, stirring to break it up, and continue cooking until the meat is completely browned. Mix in the remaining ingredients, then reduce the heat to low and simmer for 25 to 30 minutes, allowing the flavors to "marry."

continued

NOTE: You can spoon this right out of the pot onto hot dogs as they come off the grill or, if you're planning on grilling a little later, transfer it to a disposable aluminum pan, cover, and keep refrigerated. It can be easily reheated on the grill by placing the container, covered with aluminum foil, on a grill preheated to medium heat. Heat for 10 minutes, stirring occasionally. While the sauce is heating, grill hot dogs for 5 to 8 minutes, until browned and heated through. Place hot dog rolls cut-side down on the grill for 1 to 2 minutes, until lightly toasted. Then assemble the hot dogs, topping them with the sauce.

Grilled Hot Dogs

6 to 8 hot dogs

Let's be frank—at times we all crave the basics, and on the grill the winner certainly has to be the hot dog. So here are a few tips for grilling the perfect hot dog . . .

6 to 8 hot dogs (about 1 pound)
6 to 8 hot dog rolls

Preheat the grill to medium-high heat. Place the hot dogs across the grill rack and grill for 5 to 7 minutes, turning occasionally, until browned on the outside and hot throughout. Open the rolls and place the cut sides on the grill for 1 to 2 minutes, until lightly toasted. Place the hot dogs on the rolls and add your favorite toppings.

NOTE: Some people like their hot dogs lightly grilled and others like 'em bursting and well charred. See pages xxxii–xxxiii for topping suggestions.

45

Breakfast on the Grill

4 sandwiches

Breakfast is my favorite meal, and since cooking on the grill is so easy, I like making this quick breakfast for the gang. We all look forward to our special weekend grilled breakfasts, which we enjoy together on the patio.

1 to 1¼ pounds mild bulk pork sausage
2 hard-boiled eggs, sliced
4 slices American or Cheddar cheese
4 English muffins, split and toasted

Preheat the grill to medium heat. Divide the sausage into 4 equal amounts and make 4 patties, flattening them so they are ½ inch thick. Grill them for 5 to 6 minutes per side, or until the patties are cooked through and no pink remains. While the sausage is still on the grill, place 2 to 3 slices of egg, then a slice of cheese on top of each patty. Remove the sausage patties from the heat, place on the English muffins, and serve immediately.

NOTE: No English muffins? No problem! Use bagels, pitas, or toast!

State Fair Sausage, Peppers, and Onions

4 sandwiches

If you've ever been to a county or state fair, you know the incomparable smell of sausage, peppers, and onions on the grill. Want to relive those great smells and tastes right at home?

¼ cup vegetable oil
1 pound hot or sweet Italian rope sausage, cut into quarters
1 large onion, cut into ¼-inch slices
3 medium to large green or red bell peppers,
cored and cut into ½-inch strips
4 hoagie or submarine rolls, split open

Preheat the grill to medium-high heat. Pour the oil into a disposable 9" × 13" aluminum pan. Place the sausage in the center of the pan. Place the onions and peppers over and around the sausage; cover the pan with aluminum foil and place it on the grill. Close the grill cover and grill for 20 minutes, tossing the sausage mixture occasionally. Remove just the sausage chunks from the pan and place them directly on the grill; cook for 5 minutes on each side to brown the outsides. Remove the sausage from the grill and place on the rolls; top with the peppers and onions.

NOTE: To add more color to your sandwiches, use a combination of red and green bell peppers.

Hot Dog Tacos

8 tacos

How 'bout adding a few South-of-the-Border ingredients to our classic American grilled hot dogs? These sure will be the talk of the picnic, 'cause your tacos will be the only ones with hot dogs instead of ground beef!

8 hot dogs
1 tablespoon dry taco seasoning mix
(from a 1.25-ounce package)
1 tablespoon vegetable oil
8 taco shells, slightly warmed
1 cup shredded iceberg lettuce
1 cup chopped tomato
1 cup (4 ounces) shredded Cheddar cheese

Preheat the grill to medium-high heat. Make a lengthwise slit almost (but not completely) through each hot dog. In a small bowl, combine the taco seasoning mix and the oil. Spread the mixture evenly into the slits in the hot dogs. Grill them cut side up for 5 to 7 minutes, then place each hot dog inside a warmed taco shell. Top with the lettuce, tomatoes, and cheese.

NOTE: Taco seasoning mix is available in the supermarket spice section or in the ethnic foods section. If you have a warming rack on your grill, heat the taco shells on it for just a few minutes. If you don't have one, just place them on the outside edge of your grill's cooking area where the heat isn't too hot.

Three-Cheese Sausage Burgers

4 burgers

This blend of cheeses makes these burgers even more special 'cause no one can ever guess what makes them taste so super. With so few ingredients, let's keep 'em guessing!

1 pound mild bulk pork sausage
¼ cup shredded Cheddar cheese
¼ cup shredded Monterey Jack cheese
2 tablespoons grated Parmesan cheese
4 hard sandwich rolls

Preheat the grill to medium heat. In a medium-sized bowl, combine all the ingredients except the rolls; mix well. Divide the mixture into 4 equal amounts, and make 4 patties. Grill them for 10 to 12 minutes, or until cooked through and no pink remains, turning them over once during grilling. Serve on the sandwich rolls.

NOTE: You might want to use ½ cup of one of the packaged shredded cheese blends that are available (like Mexican- or Italian-style), in place of the Cheddar and Monterey Jack cheeses. It's just one more way to shorten your preparation time.

Striped Maple Sausage

4 to 6 servings

Next time you're camping—or even right in your own backyard—why not start off your breakfast with a grill full of these? Even if you can't sit around the campfire, you can have that cooked-outdoors taste!

1 pound mild bulk pork sausage
1 tablespoon maple syrup, plus extra for basting

Preheat the grill to medium heat. In a medium-sized bowl, combine the sausage and the tablespoon maple syrup. Divide the mixture into 8 equal amounts and make 8 patties, flattening them well. Grill for 8 to 10 minutes, or until the sausage is cooked through and no pink remains in the center, turning them over halfway through the grilling and basting occasionally with additional maple syrup.

NOTE: Serve this with scrambled eggs cooked right on the grill in a cast-iron or other heat-resistant heavy pan. What a great way to start off your day!

Charbroiled Chicken Champions

Chicken and barbecuing go together like peas in a pod. And when you see all the ways to grill chicken that I've collected here for you . . . Wow! Here are a few pointers for making these yummy chicken recipes:

1. Before preparing chicken, rinse it thoroughly with cold water and pat dry with paper towels.
2. Wash all cutting boards, knives, utensils, and platters with hot soapy water after they have come in contact with raw chicken. This includes the platter used to carry the raw chicken to the grill; it should not be used to hold cooked food until it has been completely washed.
3. You may want to partially cook your poultry in the oven or microwave just before putting it on the grill. By doing this, you can really cut down on the grilling time.
4. Poultry is done when it is completely cooked through. To check for doneness, cut into it near the bone. Be sure that no pink remains and the juices run clear. If you have an instant-read meat thermometer, see page xxii for instructions. The temperature for cooked poultry is 185°F.

continued

51

There is no such thing as rare chicken—if it's rare, it's not completely cooked and shouldn't be eaten until it has finished cooking!

5. Use long-handled tongs and not a fork to turn chicken. If you pierce the meat, you'll lose moisture and flavor.

Charbroiled Chicken Champions

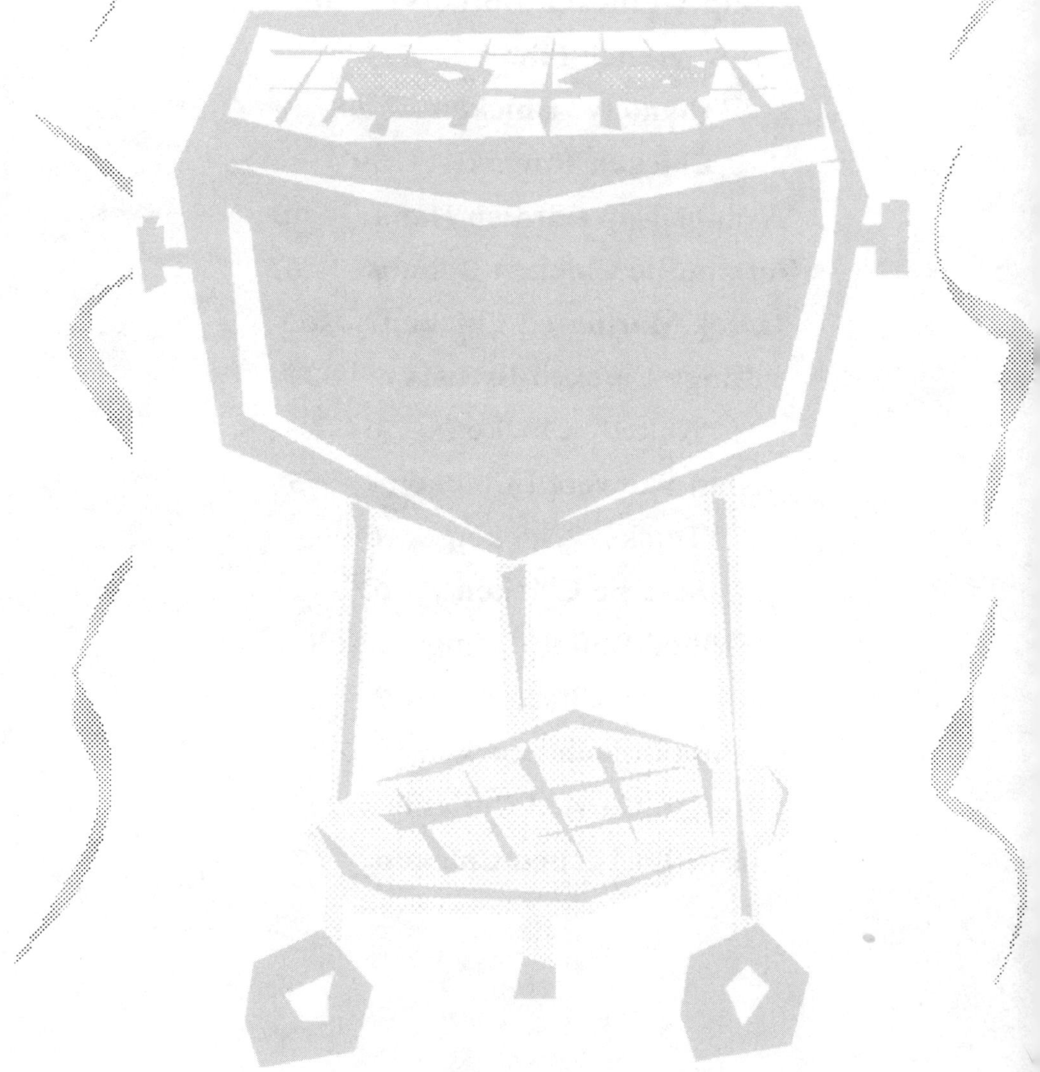

Grilled Lemon-Pepper Chicken

6 servings

All the trendy restaurants are serving this dish, and now you can make it right in your own backyard!

1 cup Italian dressing
⅔ cup powdered lemonade-flavored drink mix
2½ teaspoons pepper
6 boneless, skinless chicken breast halves

In a medium-sized bowl, mix together the dressing, lemonade mix, and pepper. Stir well and add the chicken. Cover and marinate the chicken in the refrigerator for about 8 hours, or overnight. Preheat the grill to medium-high heat. Place the chicken on the grill, discarding the marinade. Grill the chicken for 12 to 15 minutes, until a fork can be inserted into the chicken with ease and no pink remains, turning the breasts over halfway through the grilling.

Super Chicken Burgers

4 burgers

Barbecued chicken is a grilling favorite, but it usually makes for pretty messy eating. Well, it's a lot easier to eat grilled chicken this way, so why not try this new chicken on the grill?

1 to 1¼ pounds ground chicken
2 cups (8 ounces) shredded sharp Cheddar cheese
4 large mushrooms, diced
½ cup diced green bell pepper
10 large pimiento-stuffed green olives, diced
⅛ teaspoon salt
⅛ teaspoon black pepper

Preheat the grill to medium-high heat. In a large bowl, combine all the ingredients; mix well. Divide the mixture into 4 equal amounts and make 4 patties. Grill them for 8 to 12 minutes, until no pink remains and the burgers are cooked completely through, turning them over halfway through the grilling.

NOTE: Serve these on buns with your favorite condiments. Ground chicken is much blander than beef. This recipe has plenty of added flavor, but when using ground chicken (and ground turkey) in other burger recipes, remember to add extra flavor before cooking it. Try a different flavoring each time—anything from seasoned salt or other seasoning blends to garlic, chopped fresh onion, salsa, relish, or fresh basil, dill, or mint.

French Fliers

18 to 24 pieces

Thanks to the light bite of Dijon mustard and the tang of ginger and fresh garlic, you're bound to watch these fly off the serving plate!

2½ to 3 pounds split chicken wings or drumettes (see Note)
½ cup Dijon-style mustard
2 teaspoons olive oil
5 cloves garlic, chopped, or 2 teaspoons bottled
chopped garlic
½ teaspoon ground ginger
1 tablespoon Worcestershire sauce

Preheat the grill to medium-high heat. Grill the wings for 3 minutes on each side. Meanwhile, in a small bowl, combine all the remaining ingredients; mix well. Brush this mixture on the wings and grill for another 3 minutes per side, or until no pink remains.

NOTE: If you want to start with whole wings and split them yourself before cooking, split them at each joint and discard the tips. This makes them so much easier to eat.

"Thymely" Chicken

3 to 4 servings

Hectic schedule? Looking for something "thymely" to grill for dinner? Well, look no more! Here's the answer!

2 tablespoons vegetable oil
1 teaspoon garlic powder
1 teaspoon ground thyme
½ teaspoon salt
½ teaspoon pepper
1 2½- to 3-pound chicken, cut into 8 pieces

Preheat the grill to medium heat. In a small bowl, combine all the ingredients except the chicken; mix well. Rub this mixture all over the chicken, then place the chicken on the grill and close the grill cover. Grill the chicken for 35 to 40 minutes, or until the juices run clear and no pink remains, turning occasionally.

Chicken Rumaki

4 servings

Rumaki used to be found only in Asian restaurants, but now I'm going to share a simple recipe with you so that you can enjoy that unusual combination of flavors made right on your own grill.

6 boneless, skinless chicken breast halves
12 bacon slices
¾ cup ketchup
¾ cup white vinegar
1 cup firmly packed brown sugar

One hour before preparing this dish, soak 12 wooden toothpicks in water. Cut each of the chicken breast halves in half lengthwise. Wrap 1 piece of bacon securely around the width of each piece of chicken and secure with a toothpick. In a small saucepan, combine the ketchup, vinegar, and brown sugar, and bring to a boil on the stove top. Remove from heat. Preheat the grill to medium-high heat. Grill the bacon-wrapped chicken for 6 to 7 minutes per side, until the chicken is no longer pink and the bacon is crisp. Remove from the grill and serve topped with the brown sugar sauce.

NOTE: If you want this to have a real "zip," add an additional tablespoon or two of vinegar.

Wrapped-up Cornish Hens

4 to 6 servings

Fancy, fancy—and done right on the grill with hardly any work. Yup, these'll taste like you slaved all day . . . so let them think you did!

3 Cornish hens (1 to 1½ pounds each), split
⅔ cup peach preserves
2 tablespoons amaretto, or apricot or peach liqueur
½ teaspoon ground cinnamon
½ cup sliced almonds (optional)

Preheat the grill to medium-high heat. Place each hen half on a piece of heavy-duty aluminum foil. In a small bowl, combine the preserves, liqueur, and the cinnamon. Brush the mixture evenly over each hen half and wrap the halves tightly in the foil. Grill for 25 to 30 minutes, or until the juices run clear and no pink remains. Garnish with the almonds, if desired.

NOTE: Cornish hens are available in the fresh poultry department or next to the turkeys in the freezer section of your supermarket. And since they only weigh 1 to 1½ pounds, they're perfect on the grill because they're quick cookers.

Ratatouille Chicken Kebabs

4 to 6 servings

What a combination—juicy medallions of chicken skewered with eggplant and onions . . . Mmm mmm!

8 wooden or metal skewers
4 boneless, skinless chicken breast halves (about 1 pound),
cut into 1½-inch chunks
1 medium-sized eggplant, skin on, cut into 1-inch chunks
1 medium-sized onion, cut into 1-inch chunks
¾ cup Italian dressing
1 cup spaghetti sauce, warmed

If using wooden skewers, soak them in water for 15 to 20 minutes. Preheat the grill to medium-high heat. Then thread the chicken, eggplant, and onion alternately on each skewer. (Be sure to pierce the skin of the eggplant with the skewers so it won't fall apart.) Baste each kebab completely with the Italian dressing. Grill for 7 to 9 minutes, until the chicken is cooked through and no pink remains, turning the kebabs over halfway through the grilling. Discard any leftover marinade. Remove the kebabs to a serving platter and top with the warmed spaghetti sauce.

NOTE: If you want to baste the kebabs with the dressing while cooking, be careful of flare-ups from the oil in the dressing.

61

Greek Marinated Chicken

4 to 6 servings

One of my favorite chicken recipes is Greek Chicken prepared in a skillet. Now that I've discovered Greek Chicken made on the grill, I think I've got a new favorite! What do you think?

2 cloves garlic, minced
½ teaspoon dried oregano
½ cup vegetable oil
2 tablespoons lemon juice
½ teaspoon salt
¼ teaspoon pepper
6 boneless, skinless chicken breast halves

In a medium-sized bowl, combine the garlic, oregano, oil, lemon juice, salt, and pepper; mix well. Add the chicken breasts, cover, and marinate in the refrigerator for 3 to 5 hours, or overnight. Preheat the grill to medium-high heat. Grill the chicken for 15 to 18 minutes, until no pink remains and the juices run clear, turning them over halfway through the grilling.

NOTE: To give this dish even more Greek flavor, top the chicken with sliced black olives and/or some crumbled feta cheese just before serving.

Tangy Chicken Breasts

4 to 6 servings

Can you possibly make a great grilled dinner main course with just 4 ingredients? Give these a try and you'll be a believer in no time!

1½ cups apple cider vinegar
¾ cup sugar
1 tablespoon garlic powder, or 1 to 2 cloves garlic, chopped
6 chicken breast halves (bone in)

In a medium-sized bowl, combine the vinegar, sugar, and garlic. Place the chicken in a shallow pan. Pour the marinade over the chicken, cover, and marinate in the refrigerator overnight, turning occasionally. Preheat the grill to medium-high heat. Grill the chicken for 25 to 30 minutes, or until the juices run clear and no pink remains, turning the chicken frequently.

"Naked" Chicken

4 to 6 servings

With today's emphasis on health, skinless chicken is becoming more and more popular. So, here's a recipe where you remove the skin before grilling it. It's grilled "naked"!

1 teaspoon salt
¼ teaspoon black pepper
⅛ teaspoon cayenne pepper
2 teaspoons paprika
1 teaspoon garlic powder
1 teaspoon onion powder
1 2½- to 3-pound chicken, cut into quarters, skin removed

Preheat the grill to medium-high heat. In a small bowl, combine the salt, black and cayenne peppers, paprika, and garlic and onion powders; mix well. Rub the mixture all over the chicken, then wrap each quarter loosely in aluminum foil and seal well. Place the foil packets on the grill and cook the chicken for 35 to 40 minutes, until no pink remains, turning the packets over occasionally. Carefully open the packets and serve immediately.

NOTE: Why not try removing the chicken skin in other recipes in this chapter? You can still get big taste, but with less fat. Go ahead and experiment!

64

Asian Skewered Chicken

4 to 6 servings

There sure is something fun about eating chicken right off the skewer!

6 to 8 wooden or metal skewers
¼ cup soy sauce
3 tablespoons dry white wine
3 tablespoons lemon juice
2 tablespoons vegetable oil
½ teaspoon ground ginger
½ teaspoon garlic powder
¼ teaspoon onion powder
Dash of pepper
6 boneless, skinless chicken breast halves (about 1½
pounds), cut into 1½-inch chunks

If using wooden skewers, soak them in water for 15 to 20 minutes. In a medium-sized bowl, combine all of the ingredients except the chicken (and the skewers) and mix well. Add the chicken chunks, cover, and marinate for 20 to 30 minutes in the refrigerator. Preheat the grill to medium-high heat. Divide the chicken into 6 to 8 equal amounts and place the chunks on the skewers. Grill for 5 to 7 minutes, or until the chicken is cooked through and no pink remains, turning the chicken over halfway through the grilling.

"Ducky" Chicken

4 to 6 servings

You know the orange sauce found on the tables in most Chinese restaurants (not the hot mustard)? Well, some people call it sweet and sour sauce, but I call it duck sauce. And this recipe reminds me of that great taste . . . why, I think this one is "simply ducky!"

⅔ cup apricot preserves
2 tablespoons soy sauce
1 tablespoon white vinegar
1 tablespoon vegetable oil
1 tablespoon garlic powder
¼ teaspoon hot pepper sauce
6 boneless, skinless chicken breast halves

Preheat the grill to medium-high heat. In a medium-sized bowl, combine all the ingredients except the chicken. Place half of the sauce mixture in a small saucepan and warm over low heat on the stove top until the chicken is ready; place the other half in a small bowl, to be used for basting. Grill the chicken, turning once and basting with the sauce from the bowl, for 7 to 10 minutes, or until no pink remains and the juices run clear. Place the chicken on a serving platter and cover with the heated sauce.

NOTE: As I often say, I like my foods a little on the spicy side. If you do, too, then why not add an additional ¼ teaspoon of hot pepper sauce?

66

Sesame Chicken

4 to 6 servings

Sesame seeds are in so many of our favorite foods, from bagels and rolls to salads and candies, so why not team them with chicken? And on the grill, it's an unbeatable combination!

6 boneless, skinless chicken breast halves
2 tablespoons lemon juice
2 tablespoons soy sauce
¼ cup ketchup
1 tablespoon sesame oil
¼ teaspoon ground ginger
2 teaspoons brown sugar
2 tablespoons sesame seeds

Preheat the grill to medium-high heat. In a medium-sized bowl, combine all the ingredients, except the sesame seeds. Grill the chicken breasts for 10 to 13 minutes, or until no pink remains and the juices run clear, turning them over frequently and brushing them each time with the basting sauce. Remove the chicken from the grill and sprinkle with the sesame seeds before serving.

NOTE: Sesame seeds are usually found in the spice section of the supermarket.

Grilled Buffalo Wings

18 to 24 pieces

You don't have to be from Buffalo to make or eat these, but most folks from Buffalo know they pack a real punch! So get ready for a real burst of flavor. (They'll be spicy-hot, so be careful!)

2½ to 3 pounds split chicken wings or drumettes
(see Note, page 57)
¼ cup (½ stick) butter or margarine
2 tablespoons hot pepper sauce
½ teaspoon salt

Preheat the grill to medium-high heat. Grill the chicken wings for 10 to 12 minutes, until no pink remains, turning them over occasionally. Meanwhile, melt the butter in a small saucepan on the stove top and mix in the hot pepper sauce and salt. Remove from the heat and allow the mixture to cool slightly. Place in a large bowl along with the wings and toss them to coat evenly.

Taco Chicken

4 to 6 servings

With Mexican-style food still so popular, this one's a sure winner. And since it calls for the dark meat of chicken thighs, these should be really juicy!

2 tablespoons dry taco seasoning mix
(from a 1.25-ounce package)
1 teaspoon chili powder
¼ teaspoon salt
1¼ to 1½ pounds boneless, skinless chicken thighs
Regular or flavored nonstick vegetable cooking spray

Preheat the grill to medium-high heat. In a small bowl, combine the taco seasoning mix, chili powder, and salt. Lightly spray each thigh with the cooking spray. Sprinkle the seasoning mixture onto each thigh and rub evenly to coat well. Grill the chicken, turning over occasionally, for 15 to 18 minutes, or until the chicken is no longer pink and the juices run clear.

NOTE: Taco seasoning mix is available in the supermarket spice section or in the ethnic foods section.

Piña Colada Chicken

4 to 6 servings

Okay, there may not be any palm trees in your backyard or ocean breezes lightly blowing the smoke from your grill, but with this tropical treat, you'll certainly be enjoying the traditional tastes of the tropics!

6 boneless, skinless chicken breast halves
⅓ cup light corn syrup
1 can (8 ounces) crushed pineapple, undrained
2 teaspoons soy sauce
¼ cup light or dark rum
¼ cup shredded, sweetened coconut
¼ teaspoon ground ginger
¼ teaspoon salt

Place the chicken in a shallow glass baking dish. Place the remaining ingredients in a blender and blend thoroughly. Reserve ½ cup of this mixture, cover, and refrigerate until ready to use for basting. Pour the remaining marinade over the chicken, cover, and refrigerate for 3 to 4 hours, or overnight. Preheat the grill to medium-high heat. Grill the chicken for 12 to 18 minutes, basting with the reserved sauce and turning over frequently, until no pink remains and the juices run clear.

NOTE: Don't be afraid to baste this chicken lots because it'll make it that much more tropical tasting!

70

Indian Curried Cutlets

4 to 6 servings

If you think you have to go to an Indian restaurant to get the authentic tastes of Indian cooking, well... think again! This one will give you homemade rich curry flavor in a juicy turkey cutlet.

1 teaspoon curry powder
1 teaspoon onion powder
1 teaspoon ground cumin
1 teaspoon salt
1 to 1¼ pounds turkey breast cutlets (2 to 3 cutlets)
Vegetable oil for coating

Preheat the grill to medium-high heat. In a small bowl, combine the curry and onion powders, cumin, and salt. Sprinkle the cutlets with the mixture, oil your clean hands with vegetable oil, and rub the mixture lightly into the cutlets, coating them evenly. Grill the cutlets for 12 to 14 minutes, or until no pink remains and the juices run clear, turning them over halfway through the grilling.

NOTE: The larger the cutlet, the longer the grilling time. So be sure that you grill the cutlets until they're cooked all the way through.

Honey-Barbecued Chicken

3 to 4 servings

Here's a honey of a variation on barbecued chicken. This combination of ingredients makes a really crispy chicken, and I know you'll love that. (Be sure to have extra napkins on hand, because it gets pretty messy!)

1 2½- to 3-pound chicken, cut into halves,
quarters, or eighths
1 cup barbecue sauce
1 cup honey
½ teaspoon salt
½ teaspoon pepper

Preheat the oven to 350°F. Place the chicken pieces on a large cookie sheet that has been coated with nonstick vegetable cooking spray and prebake in the oven for 30 to 40 minutes. Preheat the grill to medium heat. In a small bowl, combine the remaining ingredients; mix well. Brush the mixture over the chicken and grill for 5 minutes. Turn the chicken, brushing again with the mixture, and grill for another 5 minutes, until no pink remains and the juices run clear.

NOTE: Lots of basting means lots of flavor. Also, make sure your fire isn't too hot, because the honey will caramelize in the sauce and the skin will burn.

Teriyaki Chicken

3 to 4 servings

Sure, you can buy bottled teriyaki sauce in the stores. And sure, it tastes great. But if you're out of it, or if you feel like making your own to wow the gang, here it is!

1 can (14½ ounces) ready-to-serve beef broth
¾ cup coarsely chopped onion
¼ teaspoon garlic powder
½ cup soy sauce
2 tablespoons lemon juice
3 tablespoons honey
1 2½- to 3-pound chicken, cut into quarters or eighths

In a large bowl, combine all the ingredients except the chicken and mix well. Add the chicken pieces, tossing them to coat with the sauce; cover, and refrigerate overnight. Preheat the grill to medium heat. Remove the chicken from the marinade and discard the marinade. Grill the chicken for 30 to 40 minutes, turning the chicken pieces over frequently to prevent burning, until no pink remains and the juices run clear.

NOTE: You can prebake the chicken in the oven by placing the pieces in a 9" × 13" baking pan and baking them for 25 to 30 minutes at 350°F. Then grill the chicken for just 10 to 15 minutes to crisp it up. This marinade can be used with flank steak, too. Give it a try!

73

Barbecued Wing Dings

about 32 pieces

Whether it's on chicken, burgers, or pizza, barbecue sauce is popular all around the United States. Wait till you see how easy it is to make your own barbecue specialty!

1½ cups ketchup
½ cup white vinegar
¾ cup firmly packed brown sugar
4 pounds split chicken wings or drumettes
(see Note, page 57)

Preheat the oven to 350°F. In a large bowl, combine the ketchup, vinegar, and brown sugar; mix well. Split the wings at each joint and discard the tips; rinse, then pat dry. Add the chicken to the barbecue sauce and toss to coat well. Remove the chicken, reserving the sauce, and place on a baking sheet that has been coated with nonstick vegetable cooking spray. Bake for 20 to 25 minutes. Preheat the grill to medium heat. Brush the chicken with the sauce and grill for 8 to 10 minutes, until lightly crisp and completely cooked, turning the pieces over often to prevent burning.

NOTE: Remember, a dash of hot pepper sauce will certainly add a zing to your wing!

Caesar Grilled Chicken

4 servings

Olive oil, garlic, lemon juice, and Parmesan cheese probably make you think of Caesar salad. Not this time! Instead, it's the start of a winning chicken dish that's a take-off on that favorite taste!

4 boneless, skinless chicken breast halves
⅔ cup olive oil
½ teaspoon garlic powder
¼ cup lemon juice
¼ cup grated Parmesan cheese
½ teaspoon salt
¼ teaspoon pepper
4 anchovy fillets (optional, see Note)

Cut each chicken breast half in half so that you have 8 wide strips, and place them in a medium-sized bowl. In a blender, combine the remaining ingredients, including the anchovy fillets if desired. Blend on high speed until the mixture is smooth. Pour the blended mixture over the chicken, cover, and refrigerate for 2 to 3 hours, or overnight. Preheat the grill to medium-high heat. Grill the chicken strips for 7 to 10 minutes, until the chicken is no longer pink and the juices run clear, turning the strips over occasionally.

NOTE: If you leave out the anchovies, add an extra ½ teaspoon of salt.

Lemon Coat Chicken

4 servings

A little marinade, a lot of flavor. And of course you can use fresh or bottled lemon juice—whatever makes your time in the kitchen easier.

½ cup Dijon-style mustard
¼ cup vegetable oil
¼ cup lemon juice
½ teaspoon dried dillweed
8 boneless, skinless chicken breast halves

Combine all the ingredients except the chicken in a large bowl. Add the chicken breasts and stir to coat completely. Cover and refrigerate for about 1 hour. Preheat the grill to medium-high heat and remove the chicken from the marinade, discarding excess marinade. Grill the chicken for 10 to 12 minutes, or until no pink remains, turning it over halfway through the grilling.

NOTE: This is just the right recipe for adding your own flavor touches. Each time you make it why not try a different flavoring—maybe some basil, tarragon, cumin, curry, or even chili powder?

Chicken Pesto on the Rack

4 to 6 servings

I used to think that you could make only basic foods like burgers and bar-becued chicken on the grill, but now I know it works great for fancier foods, too! This recipe is perfect for company or for a special family dinner.

6 boneless, skinless chicken breast halves
½ cup bottled pesto sauce
6 slices mozzarella cheese
⅓ cup sliced black olives (optional)

Preheat the grill to medium-high heat. Grill the chicken breasts for 12 to 15 minutes, or until no pink remains, turning them over halfway through the grilling. Spoon about 1 tablespoon pesto sauce evenly over the top of each piece of cooked chicken. Place a slice of mozzarella cheese over the pesto sauce, close the grill cover, and continue cooking for 2 to 3 minutes, or until the cheese is melted. Garnish with the black olives, if desired.

NOTE: Pesto sauce is usually available in the supermarket pro-duce or tomato sauce section.

Mouth-Watering Meats

Ahh, steak! We sure love our meats, especially when they're grilled over an open fire. And here are a few tips to help you grill them just right:

1. The more tender steak cuts are best for grilling. Try sirloin, porterhouse, strip, T-bone, rib, chuck, and filet mignon. Round, flank, and cubed steaks are very flavorful but will be easier to eat if tenderized. You can use a hand-held meat tenderizer that breaks down the tough fibers, or a seasoning type of tenderizer that is just sprinkled on—there are many kinds available.

2. The recipes in this chapter are based on ¾-inch- to 1-inch-thick steaks and chops. This is very important, because the grilling time for a steak of a different thickness would be different from what the recipe calls for. Make adjustments wherever necessary. Trim off any excess fat from the steak so that the drippings won't cause flare-ups when grilling.

3. Cut small, ⅛-inch slits around the outside edge of the steak. This should keep the steak from curling while grilling.

4. Try not to puncture steaks with tongs or a fork while turning because piercing the meat means that you'll lose flavorful juices.

continued

5.   Turn steaks and chops over just once during grilling, unless otherwise directed. About halfway through the grilling time you'll know it's time to turn a steak or chop when the juices begin to rise to the surface. If using an instant-read thermometer, cook pork to well done (170°F.), veal to well done (180°F.), and beef to the desired temperature:

Beef	
Rare	140°F.
Medium	160°F.
Well	170°F.

6.   Carve larger steaks and roasts across the grain for the most tender finished pieces.

Mouth-Watering Meats

Confetti Kebabs

6 servings

Red, yellow, green, white—wow! The colorful veggies look like confetti. And the taste is just as exciting.

6 wooden or metal skewers
1 large red bell pepper, cored, cleaned, and cut into 6 pieces
1 large yellow bell pepper, cored, cleaned,
and cut into 6 pieces
1 large green bell pepper, cored, cleaned,
and cut into 6 pieces
1 large onion, cut into 6 chunks
6 large mushrooms, cleaned
2 pounds flank steak, cut into 1½- to 2-inch pieces
½ cup Italian dressing
¼ cup pesto sauce

If using wooden skewers, soak them in water for 15 to 20 minutes. Preheat the grill to medium-high heat. In a large bowl, combine all the ingredients (except the skewers); stir to coat the meat and vegetables evenly. Alternately thread the peppers, beef, and mushrooms onto the skewers. Grill for 10 to 12 minutes, or until the beef is done to your liking.

NOTE: Ask your butcher for the thickest part of the flank steak.

Seaside Turf

4 to 5 servings

When restaurants team seafood and steak, they call it Surf and Turf. Well, in this recipe, rub seafood seasoning on steak for results that "shore" are unexpectedly tasty!

1 tablespoon seafood seasoning
2 to 2½ pounds flank steak

Preheat the grill to medium-high heat. Rub the seafood seasoning into both sides of the steak. Grill the steak for 4 minutes on each side, or until the center is cooked medium-rare to medium. Slice the steak on an angle, across the grain.

NOTE: Do not cook flank steak more than to medium-well done, as it will become very tough. There are loads of brands of seafood seasoning available. Each one is a combination of several seasonings, so this way it's easy to get a great flavor combination with very little work!

Secret Glazed Spareribs

4 to 6 servings

The secret comes from the grape jelly, 'cause when it's mixed with the other ingredients it adds an "ooh-la-la" that no one can identify!

4 to 5 pounds pork spareribs
¾ cup bottled chili sauce
½ cup grape jelly
2 teaspoons dry mustard

Place the ribs in a stockpot and cover with water. Boil, covered, for 45 minutes to 1 hour. Meanwhile, in a medium-sized bowl, combine the remaining ingredients. Preheat the grill to medium-high heat about 10 minutes before the ribs finish boiling. Place them on the grill and close the grill cover. Grill the ribs, turning them over frequently and basting them with the mixture each time they are turned, until they are browned and glazed, about 12 to 15 minutes.

Pineapple Ham Kebabs

4 to 6 servings

Why not try grilling ham, peppers, and pineapple on skewers for a whole new quick dinner taste? (I bet you'll try it again and again, even when you're not in a hurry!)

6 to 8 wooden or metal skewers
1 pound ham steak, cut into 1-inch cubes
1 can (20 ounces) pineapple chunks, drained,
with ⅔ cup juice reserved
2 large red or green bell peppers, cored, cleaned,
and cut into 1-inch squares
½ cup firmly packed brown sugar

If using wooden skewers, soak them in water for 15 to 20 minutes. Then, on each skewer, alternately thread chunks of ham, pineapple, and bell pepper. Place the skewers in a 9" × 13" baking dish. In a medium-sized glass bowl, combine the reserved pineapple juice and the brown sugar. Stir until the sugar dissolves. If the sugar does not readily dissolve, you can place the glass bowl in the microwave and heat for 30 to 40 seconds on high power, then stir it again. Pour the mixture over the kebabs, cover, and refrigerate for about 30 minutes, turning occasionally. Preheat the grill to medium-high heat. Grill the kebabs for 9 to 12 minutes, basting with the excess marinade, and turning frequently. Remove the kebabs from the grill when the peppers are cooked and the edges of the meat, peppers, and pineapple are crispy. Discard any leftover marinade.

Jamaican Beef

4 to 6 servings

Jamaican rum, island breezes, blue waters . . . yup, those are what I think of when I make this recipe. And so will you!

½ cup vegetable oil
2 tablespoons bottled steak sauce
½ teaspoon white vinegar
2½ tablespoons brown sugar
⅓ cup peanut butter
1 tablespoon soy sauce
¼ cup flaked coconut
¼ teaspoon garlic powder
¼ teaspoon salt
1½ pounds bottom round steak
4 to 6 wooden or metal skewers

In a blender, combine all the ingredients except the steak (and the skewers); blend thoroughly. Cut the steak into ¼-inch-wide strips and place in a medium-sized bowl; add the blended mixture and stir to coat evenly. Cover and refrigerate for 1 to 2 hours, or overnight. Preheat the grill to medium-high heat and, if using wooden skewers, soak in water for 15 to 20 minutes. Thread the steak strips lengthwise on the skewers, 3 to 4 strips per skewer. Grill for 6 to 8 minutes, turning frequently.

NOTE: You can also use boneless, skinless chicken breasts. Be sure to cook them until done and no pink remains.

Country Grilled Steak

4 servings

Crispy on the outside, tender and juicy on the inside, and *the down-home taste we all love.*

½ cup yellow cornmeal
2 teaspoons chili powder
½ teaspoon salt
½ teaspoon pepper
4 rib eye steaks (8 to 10 ounces each)

Preheat the grill to medium-high heat. In a medium-sized bowl, combine all the ingredients except the steaks; mix well. Dip each steak into the mixture and pat the breading firmly into the steak, coating evenly. Grill the steaks for 10 to 12 minutes, or until desired doneness, turning them over once.

NOTE: Rib eye steaks are my personal favorite for this recipe, but why not try porterhouse or strip steaks?

Hot Striped Steak

4 servings

Sometimes the most basic things on the grill are the best. How do you get the stripes? Grill it over a hot fire and the grill racks will do the rest.

½ cup bottled steak sauce
½ teaspoon garlic powder
1 tablespoon hot pepper sauce
2 sirloin steaks (1 pound each)

Preheat the grill to medium-high heat. In a large bowl, combine the steak sauce, garlic powder, and hot pepper sauce; mix well. Add the steaks and stir to coat evenly with the sauce. Let sit for 5 minutes. Grill the steaks for 10 to 12 minutes, or until desired doneness, turning them over halfway through the grilling.

NOTE: Try this steak topped with "Steak Out" Veggies (page 129).

Beefy Liver and Onions

4 servings

Want the taste of yesteryear with the ease of today? Go ahead and re-create the yummy flavors of liver and onions on the grill.

1 teaspoon salt, plus extra for sprinkling
½ teaspoon pepper
½ teaspoon ground cumin
½ teaspoon onion powder
1 teaspoon garlic powder
1 to 1¼ pounds beef liver, cut into 4 slices ¼ to ⅓ inch thick
2 large sweet onions, cut into slices ½ inch thick
Olive oil for brushing

Preheat the grill to medium-high heat. In a small bowl, combine the 1 teaspoon of salt with the pepper, cumin, and onion and garlic powders. Sprinkle over the liver. Grill, turning once, for 10 to 15 minutes, or until desired doneness. While the liver is grilling, brush the onion slices with olive oil and sprinkle with salt. Grill the onions for 10 to 15 minutes, or until brown and slightly soft, turning them over occasionally. Serve over the liver.

Beef Stew Kebabs

4 servings

Beef stew on the grill?! Why not? It's your perfect answer to late-summer grilling, when the nights get cooler and the food gets heartier.

8 wooden or metal skewers
1 teaspoon salt
1 teaspoon pepper
1½ teaspoons onion powder
1½ teaspoons garlic powder
1 to 1¼ pounds chuck roast, cut into 1½- to 2-inch pieces
2 cans (15 ounces each) whole white potatoes, drained
1 package (16 ounces) frozen whole baby carrots, thawed
1 can or jar (10 to 12 ounces) beef or brown gravy, warmed

If using wooden skewers, soak them in water for 15 to 20 minutes. Preheat the grill to medium-high heat. In a small bowl, combine the salt, pepper, and onion and garlic powders. Place the meat, potatoes, and carrots in a large bowl and add the seasoning mixture, tossing to coat the meat and vegetables evenly. Thread the meat, potatoes, and carrots alternately on the skewers and grill for 10 to 12 minutes, turning the skewers over occasionally, until the meat reaches the desired doneness. Remove the kebabs to a platter and top with the warm gravy.

Garden Herb Steak

4 servings

Talk about bursting with flavor . . . ! With this combination of herbs, the taste is like a walk in the garden.

2 teaspoons dried basil
½ teaspoon salt
½ teaspoon pepper
2 teaspoons parsley flakes
1 teaspoon dried dillweed
4 strip or rib eye steaks (8 to 10 ounces each)
Regular or flavored nonstick vegetable cooking spray

Preheat the grill to medium high. In a small bowl, combine the basil, salt, pepper, parsley flakes, and dill; mix well. Spray both sides of the steaks with the nonstick vegetable spray. Then sprinkle the spice mixture evenly over the steaks, rubbing well to coat. Grill for 10 to 12 minutes, or until desired doneness, turning the steaks over halfway through the grilling.

NOTE: Dried herbs are great for getting flavor in a jiffy, but if you have the time, try using 2 tablespoons fresh chopped basil, 2 tablespoons fresh chopped parsley, and 1 tablespoon fresh chopped dillweed along with the salt and pepper.

European Steak Roll-ups

4 servings

You ask why this is called European? It's because a touch of red wine adds a French flair. Then there's the Italian dressing . . . and the results are four-star delicious!

1 cup Italian dressing
¼ cup dry red wine
4 bottom round steaks (4 to 5 ounces each), ⅛ inch thick

In a shallow dish, combine the dressing and the wine. Add the steaks, turning to coat completely. Cover and refrigerate for 1 to 2 hours. Preheat the grill to medium-high heat. Remove the steaks from the marinade, discarding the excess marinade. Roll up each steak slice (to about the size of a hot dog) and place across the racks of the preheated grill, seam side down. Grill the steaks for 5 minutes, turning occasionally.

NOTE: To complete this with a French flair, serve it with some thinly sliced cooked red potatoes; or, to bring out the Italian in you, serve it with cooked pasta.

Parmesan Steak

4 servings

Light up the grill, toss on the steaks, and before they eat, make sure you have 'em say "Cheese!"

2 cups creamy Parmesan dressing
2 tablespoons vegetable oil
2 teaspoons soy sauce
4 rib, strip, or round steaks (10 ounces each)

Combine all the ingredients except the steaks in a small bowl. Place the steaks in a large resealable plastic bag and pour the mixture over them. Seal the bag and refrigerate for 2 hours. Preheat the grill to medium-high heat. Grill the steaks for about 8 to 10 minutes per side, or until desired doneness.

NOTE: With all the dressings on the market today, you can certainly use a variation of regular Parmesan dressing, like one with ground peppercorns or herbs.

Rub-a-Dub Pork

4 to 6 servings

Mix, rub, and grill. Now, that's easy, that's quick, and that's my kind of meal!

¼ cup ketchup
1 tablespoon prepared mustard
1 teaspoon brown sugar
2 pounds pork tenderloins

Preheat the grill to medium-high heat. In a medium-sized bowl, combine all the ingredients except the pork; mix well. Brush the mixture over the pork and grill for 10 minutes per side, or until completely cooked through.

NOTE: You'll find some very attractive prices on pork tenderloins, so buy several and keep them on hand in the freezer for this quick, throw-on-the-grill favorite.

Down-Home Ribs

4 servings

We all have our own favorite comfort foods, and what can be more down-home-comforting than ribs? I save them for special times, so to me, these are homey comfort.

¼ cup Dijon-style mustard
¼ cup mayonnaise
¼ cup balsamic vinegar
½ teaspoon garlic powder
1 tablespoon light brown sugar
2½ to 3 pounds country-style pork ribs

Preheat the grill to medium-high heat. In a small bowl, combine all the ingredients except the ribs. Grill the ribs for 15 to 20 minutes, basting with the glaze and turning them over occasionally.

NOTE: My family likes a batch of coleslaw and some crusty bread with these. I bet your gang will, too!

Sicilian Pork Chops

4 servings

You'll know you're in for a treat when you smell the garlic in these! Mmm—they'll come running.

¼ cup olive oil
1 teaspoon garlic powder
3 tablespoons Italian-style dry bread crumbs
½ teaspoon salt
4 pork chops (6 to 8 ounces each)

Preheat the grill to medium-high heat. Combine all the ingredients except the chops in a medium-sized bowl; mix well. Dip the chops in the mixture and rub until the chops are well coated. Grill for 8 to 10 minutes on each side, or until completely cooked through.

NOTE: If you want, you can serve the chops topped with a cup of warmed spaghetti sauce.

Gooey Country Ribs

3 to 4 servings

Make sure you've got plenty of napkins nearby, 'cause these are so gooey and finger lickin'.

½ cup maple syrup
2 teaspoons Worcestershire sauce
1 teaspoon hot pepper sauce
1½ to 1¾ pounds country-style pork ribs

Preheat the grill to medium-high heat. Combine all the ingredients except the ribs in a small bowl; mix well. Grill the ribs for 15 to 20 minutes, or until no pink remains, basting with the sauce and turning the ribs over occasionally.

NOTE: I like to be sure these are cooked to well done because the syrup will caramelize and have lots of crispy flavor.

98

Bourbon Steak

4 servings

Don't worry about the alcohol in this dish because it cooks off, leaving its rich flavor behind.

2 teaspoons prepared mustard
½ cup bottled steak sauce
¼ cup bourbon whiskey
1 tablespoon honey
4 rib, strip, round, or chuck steaks (10 ounces each)

Combine all the ingredients except the steaks in a baking dish or resealable plastic bag; mix well. Add the steaks; cover (or seal) and refrigerate for 2 hours, or overnight. Preheat the grill to medium-high heat. Grill the steaks for 12 to 15 minutes, or until desired doneness, turning them over halfway through the grilling.

NOTE: You can use four 10-ounce steaks or two 1¼-pound steaks—the choice is yours. But remember: The thicker the steak, the longer the cooking time.

99

Apricot-Glazed Ham

4 servings

Why wait for a special occasion to have ham? Make it right on the grill anytime!

1 can (8 ounces) pineapple slices, drained,
with ¼ cup juice reserved
½ cup apricot preserves
1 teaspoon dry mustard
¼ cup dark raisins
4 ham steaks (7 to 8 ounces each), cut ½ inch thick

Preheat the grill to medium-high heat. In a disposable aluminum pie plate, combine the reserved pineapple juice, apricot preserves, mustard, and raisins. Cook on the grill, stirring frequently, for 4 to 6 minutes until the preserves melt. Grill the ham steaks for 10 to 12 minutes, turning them over occasionally. Grill the pineapple slices for 5 to 6 minutes, turning them over halfway through the grilling. Serve the ham with the pineapple slices and top with the sauce.

NOTE: Serve this with rice so you don't miss any of this yummy sauce!

Cracked Pepper
Veal Chops

4 servings

Most of us love pepper. After all, it's almost always just a shake away. But when we add it to our meat before grilling, watch out! The flavor just explodes!

1 teaspoon salt
2 teaspoons cracked peppercorns or coarse ground black pepper
1 teaspoon crushed red pepper
2 teaspoons dry mustard
2 teaspoons garlic powder
3 tablespoons vegetable oil
4 veal chops (8 ounces each)

Preheat the grill to medium-high heat. In a small bowl, combine the salt, black and red peppers, mustard, and garlic powder. Stir in the oil to form a paste. Rub the mixture over the chops until well coated. Grill the chops for 12 to 15 minutes, or to desired doneness, turning them over halfway through the cooking.

NOTE: If you don't have peppercorns, try to use black pepper that you grind yourself right from the peppermill. That'll give your chops that really fresh-cracked-pepper taste.

Country Ribs

3 to 4 servings

You don't have to live in the country to make these... In fact, I know so many "city folks" who like these that maybe I should call them "City Ribs"?!

½ cup barbecue sauce
¾ cup sweet-and-sour sauce
1 tablespoon hot pepper sauce
1½ to 2 pounds country-style pork ribs

Preheat the grill to medium-high heat. In a medium-sized bowl, combine all the ingredients except the ribs; mix well. Baste the ribs with the sauce and grill them for 10 minutes. Turn the ribs, baste again, and grill for another 10 minutes, or until completely cooked through.

NOTE: Country-style ribs are meatier than spareribs, but you still might want to make a double batch because they disappear so fast!

Caesar Veal Chops

4 servings

On your mark, get set, grill! With the big flavor and these tender chops, everybody will come racing to the table!

1 package (1.2 ounces) dry Caesar dressing mix
2 tablespoons olive oil
4 veal chops (8 to 10 ounces each)

Preheat the grill to medium-high heat. In a small bowl, combine the dressing mix and oil. Coat both sides of the veal chops with the mixture and grill the chops for 12 to 15 minutes, turning them over once during the grilling.

NOTE: To make these extra fancy, try squeezing the juice from a lemon over the chops right before they come off the grill.

Orchard Pork Chops

4 servings

Apples and pork—what a combination! And with the taste from the grill, it's even better!

½ cup olive oil
⅓ cup apple cider vinegar
1½ cups apple juice
2 cloves garlic
1 teaspoon salt
½ teaspoon white pepper
4 loin pork chops (6 to 8 ounces each)

Combine all the ingredients except the chops in a large bowl. Mix well and add the chops, coating completely. Cover and refrigerate overnight, turning occasionally. Preheat the grill to medium heat. Remove the chops from the marinade, discarding any excess. Grill the chops for 8 to 10 minutes per side, or until completely cooked through.

Minted Lamb Chops

4 servings

*I grew up having mint jelly with broiled lamb chops . . . It's a natural combo!
I'm taking that a step further now by grilling the chops and topping them
with a minty sauce. Wow! You've gotta try it!*

½ cup mint jelly
2 tablespoons canned chopped chilies, drained
2 tablespoons butter or margarine
6 to 8 center-cut lamb chops (4 to 6 ounces each)

Preheat the grill to medium-high heat. In a disposable aluminum
pie pan, combine the jelly, chilies, and butter. Place on the preheated grill and heat for 4 to 6 minutes, until the jelly melts, stirring occasionally. While the sauce is heating, grill the chops for
12 to 15 minutes, or until desired doneness, turning them over
once during the grilling. Remove from the grill and serve topped
with the sauce.

Meat Loaf on the Grill

6 to 8 servings

Meat loaf on the grill?? Yup! I know most of us have grown up on moist, flavorful meat loaf made in Mom's oven, but we can still get the same taste (maybe even better!) on our grills.

2 pounds ground beef
1½ cups dry bread crumbs
2 eggs
¾ cup water
⅓ cup ketchup
½ teaspoon garlic powder
½ teaspoon salt
½ teaspoon pepper

Preheat the grill to medium-high heat. In a large bowl, combine all the ingredients; mix well. Shape into 2 loaves, each about 1 inch thick. Place in a hinged grill basket that has been coated with nonstick vegetable cooking spray. Place on the grill and cook, turning once, for 20 to 30 minutes, until the loaves are firm and no pink remains. (Cooking time will depend on the thickness of your loaves and the heat of your grill.)

NOTE: Very lean ground turkey or chicken works great, too—but be sure to increase your seasonings to almost double the amount used here when using turkey or chicken.

Mustardy Pork Chops

4 servings

The mustard does the trick here, 'cause it adds so much flavor . . . simply!

½ cup vegetable oil
¼ cup apple cider vinegar
2 tablespoons Dijon-style mustard
1 teaspoon salt
½ teaspoon pepper
4 pork chops (6 to 8 ounces each)

In a small bowl, combine all the ingredients except the chops; mix well. Place the chops in a single layer in a shallow baking dish. Pour the marinade over the chops and let sit for 2 hours, or overnight. Preheat the grill to medium-high heat. Grill the chops for 12 to 15 minutes, or until no pink remains, turning them over halfway through the grilling.

NOTE: My preference is to use Dijon-style mustard, but I've tried these with plain yellow mustard and the results are still lip-smackin' good.

Baseball Park Steak

4 servings

We've all heard the vendors at the ballpark shouting, "Cold beer here!" "Get your roasted peanuts here!" Well, now we can have those great tastes together with our grilled steak. This one's a real champion!

1 bottle (12 ounces) beer
1 cup shelled peanuts, with or without salt
½ teaspoon salt (if using unsalted nuts)
4 strip steaks (6 to 8 ounces each)

In a blender, on high speed, combine the beer, peanuts, and salt, if using. Blend until smooth. Place the steaks in a shallow dish and pour the beer mixture over them. Cover and refrigerate for 2 to 3 hours or overnight, turning occasionally. Preheat the grill to medium-high heat. Grill the steaks for 10 to 12 minutes, or until desired doneness, turning them over halfway through the grilling.

Salted Eye of the Round Barbecue

8 to 10 servings

This is one of my most-requested meat recipes. It's a particular method of cooking eye of the round where the meat is cooked directly on barbecue coals or on the lava rocks of a gas grill. It takes a little more cooking time than my other recipes, but boy, it's sure worth it! (You need to follow the directions carefully and give it your complete attention.)

1 eye of the round roast (4 to 5 pounds)
4 cups kosher (coarse) salt

Remove the grate from your grill, then preheat it to high heat. (With a charcoal grill, this means letting the fire go until there is a good bed of red-hot coals.) Meanwhile, tear off a piece of waxed paper large enough to wrap the roast completely. (Use two sheets if necessary, and overlap them.) Place the waxed paper flat on a countertop, place the roast in the center, and pour the kosher salt over the meat. Use your clean hands to spread the salt evenly all over the meat, until it is completely covered and white. **Do not be afraid to use too much salt.** Wrap the meat with the waxed paper as completely as you can, so that all of the salt stays inside the wrapper. Here's where you need to be careful: Place the waxed-paper-wrapped meat directly on the hot coals or lava rocks and stand back immediately because the waxed paper will instantly flame up and burn away. Leave the grill cover off. Let the meat cook for 35 to 40

minutes on one side. Then use two long-handled meat forks or long-handled tongs to flip the meat, and cook it for 30 to 35 minutes more on the second side. Again, **do not cover the grill**. Carefully remove the meat from the coals and scrape off any remaining bits of waxed paper and salt. (The outside of the meat will be black.) Place the meat in something shallow for carving, so that the juices can be saved for serving over it. Carve the roast across the grain in thin (about ¼-inch) slices.

NOTE: If you follow the directions carefully, you'll end up with a range of slices from medium-rare to well done, so that everybody can have moist and delicious roast beef done their own perfect way. **Please be sure to keep children away from your fire.**

Sizzling Seafood

A lot of people don't like cooking fish at home because of the smell. Well, cooking it on the grill is the answer! It's super because there should be no lingering aroma . . . and the taste is unbelievably rich and satisfying!

1. Always select fresh fish or fish that has been flash-frozen at sea. If you're using fish that has been frozen, let it thaw overnight in the refrigerator.
2. Before preparing fish, always wash it with cold water and pat it dry with paper towels.
3. Meaty fish steaks, like tuna, salmon, and halibut, can be grilled right on the grill rack. More delicate fish like whiting, cod, and haddock work best cooked in hinged grill baskets (see page xxi). The baskets make grilling fish a breeze because they help keep it all together. (You'll rush to grill fish again and again!)
4. To prevent the fish from sticking, spray the **cold** hinged grill baskets or the grill racks with regular or flavored nonstick vegetable cooking spray before lighting the grill. If you forget, carefully remove the rack (it will be hot, so be careful!) from the grill, wait for it to cool a bit, spray it away from the heat, and carefully replace it on the grill.
5. Do not overcook fish, as it will fall apart when overdone. Usually it should be cooked for no more than 10 minutes per inch at its thickest part, but this will vary somewhat depending upon the heat of your fire.

Sizzling Seafood

Sweet and Spicy Shrimp

4 servings

Yes, I mean Sweet and Spicy, not sweet and sour. And it's a combination that'll really wake up your taste buds!

4 wooden or metal skewers
1 to 1¼ pounds large uncooked shrimp, peeled and deveined
(20 to 25 shrimp)
½ cup apricot preserves
¼ teaspoon cayenne pepper
1 teaspoon vegetable oil
½ teaspoon soy sauce

If using wooden skewers, soak them in water for 15 to 20 minutes. Preheat the grill to medium-high heat. Thread 6 shrimp on each skewer; set aside. Combine the remaining ingredients in a small bowl. Grill the shrimp for 6 to 8 minutes, basting both sides with the apricot mixture about 3 times during the grilling.

NOTE: I recommend leaving the tails on the shrimp when you peel them because it makes them easier to eat—and they look great that way, too!

Crusted Salmon

4 servings

There's so much to like about salmon—the rich taste, the bright color, the firm texture—no wonder it's so popular! And the mayonnaise is the secret here, because when it's grilled it forms a crispy crust.

⅓ cup mayonnaise
1 teaspoon dried dillweed
1 tablespoon lemon juice
½ teaspoon minced garlic (1 to 2 cloves)
½ teaspoon salt
¼ teaspoon pepper
4 salmon steaks or fillets (6 to 8 ounces each)

Spray the **cold** grill racks with nonstick vegetable cooking spray. Preheat the grill to medium heat. In a small bowl, combine all the ingredients except the salmon; mix well. Rinse the salmon with cold water and pat dry with a paper towel. Divide the mixture evenly among the salmon, spreading it on both sides. Grill the salmon for 10 to 12 minutes, or until the fish flakes easily with a fork and is cooked through in the center. Serve immediately.

NOTE: When I've got it, I like to use a tablespoon of fresh chopped dillweed in place of the dried dillweed.

Gumbo on the Grill

4 to 6 servings

Watch out, New Orleans! Now we can make hearty gumbo on the grill—yes, right on our grills! Don't wait till Mardi Gras to try this Southern specialty.

> 1 can (14½ ounces) stewed tomatoes, undrained
> 1 can (6½ ounces) chopped clams, undrained
> 1 can (4½ ounces) tiny whole shrimp, undrained
> ½ cup medium salsa
> ½ cup instant rice

Preheat the grill to medium-high heat. In an 8-inch square disposable aluminum pan, combine all the ingredients; mix well. Cover with aluminum foil and place on the grill. Close the grill cover and cook the gumbo for about 8 minutes; then stir it, re-cover it, and cook for another 2 to 4 minutes, or until the rice is cooked.

NOTE: Stir in ½ cup water when reheating any leftover gumbo because the liquid will be absorbed while it sits overnight.

Rack 'Em Up Cod

4 servings

I love cod because it's such a mild-flavored fish. That means it's perfect for teaming with your favorite seasonings. Try this winning combination of flavors, then if you like experimenting, change the spices to your own favorites.

1 tablespoon vegetable oil
½ teaspoon dried dillweed
½ teaspoon chili powder
½ teaspoon garlic powder
½ teaspoon paprika
¼ teaspoon salt
¼ teaspoon pepper
1½ pounds fresh or frozen cod fillets, thawed if frozen

Preheat the grill to medium-high heat. Coat a hinged grill basket with nonstick vegetable cooking spray. In a small bowl, combine all the ingredients except the cod; mix well. Rinse the fish with cold water and pat dry with a paper towel. Cover the fish with the mixture, rubbing all of it onto the fish. Grill the fish in the grill basket for 9 to 11 minutes, depending on the thickness, or until the fish flakes easily with a fork, turning the basket over occasionally.

NOTE: This works well with whiting or haddock, too.

Simple Teriyaki Tuna

4 servings

Did you think that tuna fish comes just in a can? Well, it doesn't! Don't miss out on this big taste in fresh seafood!

⅓ cup soy sauce
2 tablespoons vegetable oil
2 tablespoons brown sugar
2 cloves garlic, minced
4 tuna steaks (6 to 8 ounces each)

In a large bowl, combine all the ingredients except the tuna; mix well. Rinse the tuna with cold water and pat dry with a paper towel. Add the tuna, cover, and refrigerate for 20 to 30 minutes, turning over once. Spray the **cold** grill racks with non-stick vegetable cooking spray. Preheat the grill to medium-high heat. Grill the tuna steaks for 8 to 10 minutes, or until desired doneness, turning them over occasionally.

NOTE: Tuna steaks can be cooked like beef—to medium, medium-well, or well done.

117

"Blue" Trout

4 servings

It's grilled . . . no, no, it's poached . . . or is it baked?! Well, however it gets cooked here, we can call it super-duper. It's like cooking individual casseroles in minutes!

4 trout fillets (4 ounces each)
1 tablespoon plus 1 teaspoon butter
½ teaspoon salt
¼ cup milk
¼ cup crumbled blue cheese

Preheat the grill to medium-high heat. Rinse the fish with cold water and pat dry with a paper towel. Roll up each trout fillet and place each in one of the cups of a disposable aluminum muffin tin. Top each roll-up with a teaspoon of butter, ⅛ teaspoon salt, a tablespoon of milk, and a tablespoon of blue cheese. Place the muffin tin on the grill; close the cover and cook for 10 to 12 minutes, or until the fish is hot and cooked through.

NOTE: If you don't like blue cheese, you can certainly use any of your favorites.

Fisherman's Grill

4 servings

The next time you're fishing for an idea for dinner, pull out this recipe . . . your dinner crowd will be hooked!

1 cup cheese crackers
¼ teaspoon dry mustard
½ teaspoon garlic powder
¼ teaspoon salt
¼ teaspoon white pepper
⅓ cup shredded Cheddar cheese
1 to 1¼ pounds fresh or frozen whiting fillets,
thawed if frozen
3 tablespoons melted butter or margarine, divided

Spray the **cold** grill racks with nonstick vegetable cooking spray. Preheat the grill to medium-high heat. In a medium-sized bowl, crush the cheese crackers into crumbs. Add the mustard, garlic powder, salt, pepper, and Cheddar cheese; mix well. Rinse the fish with cold water and pat dry with a paper towel. Spread 1 tablespoon of the melted butter on the bottom of an 8-inch square disposable aluminum pan; place the fish in the butter, then spread the crumb mixture evenly over the fish. Drizzle the remaining butter over the crumb topping. Grill the fish for 10 to 15 minutes, depending on the thickness, or until the fish flakes easily with a fork and is cooked through.

NOTE: If you prefer, you can use haddock or cod instead of whiting.

Trout Parmigiana

4 servings

You've had Veal Parmigiana topped with rich tomato sauce and melted mozzarella cheese? Well, here's the same idea made with trout. Boy, will you be amazed by the results!

4 trout fillets (4 ounces each)
¼ cup spaghetti sauce
¼ cup shredded mozzarella cheese
1 teaspoon grated Parmesan cheese

Preheat the grill to medium-high heat. Rinse the fish with cold water and pat dry with a paper towel. Roll up each trout fillet and place each roll on end in one of the cups of a disposable aluminum muffin tin. Top each with a tablespoon of spaghetti sauce, a tablespoon of mozzarella cheese, and ¼ teaspoon Parmesan cheese. Place the muffin tin on the grill; close the cover and cook for 10 to 12 minutes, or until the fish is hot and bubbling and cooked through.

NOTE: Since most of us have bottled spaghetti sauce on hand, why not change the flavor of this dish by using different types of spaghetti sauce? Go with zesty spices one time, garden veggies another, and hearty it up with your own homemade sauce or a homemade-style bottled sauce another time.

Steamers on the Grill

2 dozen

These are like clams at a clam bake, with a hint of lemon. And no, you don't need a fancy clam steamer—just an aluminum pan and your grill! With the high temperature of the grill, they open up and are ready to eat in minutes.

1 cup water
2 lemons, cut into quarters
2 dozen Mahogany, littleneck, or cherrystone clams,
soaked in ice water for 30 minutes

Preheat the grill to medium-high heat. Pour the water into a disposable 9" × 13" aluminum pan and add the lemon quarters. Place the clams in the water and cover with aluminum foil. Place the pan on the grill and close the cover. Grill for 7 to 9 minutes, or until the clams open wide. **Discard any clams that do not open by themselves.**

NOTE: Dip the cooked clams in melted butter, but be careful when picking them up because the liquid from inside the clams will be very hot.

Grilled Red Snapper

4 servings

Some people avoid cooking fish because they think it's "too much work." Well, not anymore! In fact, it's even better cooked on the grill 'cause this way, there's no odor in the kitchen!

1 tablespoon curry powder
1 tablespoon ground cumin
½ teaspoon salt
½ teaspoon pepper
1 teaspoon garlic powder
4 red snapper fillets (about 6 ounces each)
¼ cup vegetable oil

Preheat the grill to medium-high heat. In a small bowl, combine the curry powder, cumin, salt, pepper, and garlic powder; mix well. Rinse the fish with cold water and pat dry with a paper towel. Rub a tablespoon of the oil on each piece of fish, then rub the spice mixture into both sides of the fish, coating it evenly. Place the fish in a hinged grill basket that has been coated with nonstick vegetable cooking spray. Grill the fish for 7 to 9 minutes, or until cooked through and firm to the touch, turning the basket over once during cooking.

NOTE: If you don't have a hinged grill basket, before preheating the grill, coat the grill racks with nonstick vegetable cooking spray. Then place the fish skin side up on the grill first. That way, when you turn it over, it is less likely that the fish will stick to the grill.

Nutty Grilled Flounder

3 to 4 servings

Awesome . . . that's the word that came to my lips after I first tasted this nutty grilled concoction. What do you think?

2 cups finely chopped walnuts
1 teaspoon salt
½ teaspoon cayenne pepper
1 to 1¼ pounds flounder fillets
¼ cup (½ stick) melted butter or margarine

Preheat the grill to medium-high heat. In a medium-sized bowl, combine the walnuts, salt, and cayenne pepper; mix well. Rinse the fish with cold water and pat dry with a paper towel. Place the melted butter in a small bowl; dip the flounder into the butter, then the nut mixture, coating the fish completely. Place the fish in a hinged grill basket that has been coated with non-stick vegetable cooking spray. Grill the fish for 5 to 7 minutes, or until the fish flakes easily with a fork and is cooked through, turning the basket over occasionally.

NOTE: You can "fancy" this up by using pecans instead of walnuts . . . or maybe you'd prefer almonds or peanuts? Whatever's your fancy!

Swordfish Scampi

4 to 6 servings

We've all seen Shrimp Scampi on restaurant menus. (It's shrimp smothered in garlic, butter, and lemon.) When swordfish is prepared this way on the grill, you get a real seafood treat!

¼ cup (½ stick) melted butter or margarine
1 teaspoon garlic powder
1 tablespoon lemon juice
1¼ to 1½ pounds fresh or frozen swordfish steaks,
thawed if frozen

Spray the **cold** grill racks with nonstick vegetable cooking spray. Preheat the grill to medium-high heat. In a small bowl, combine the melted butter, garlic powder, and lemon juice; mix well. Rinse the fish with cold water and pat dry with a paper towel. Brush the mixture on the fish and grill the fish for 10 to 12 minutes, or until cooked through, turning the fish over occasionally and brushing it with the butter mixture each time.

NOTE: I like to give the fish an extra squeeze of lemon while it's on the grill. You can also use any steak-type of fish instead of swordfish—you know, like halibut or salmon.

125

From Garden to Grill

The grill's already going and dinner is cooking . . . but you're not sure what to have with it! Well, why not cook your dinner "go-alongs" right on the grill? Yup, potatoes and veggies can easily share your grill, which means less cleanup and lots of smiles around the table!

1. Plan ahead, if possible. If you do, then you'll be ready to put your different courses on the grill at the right times so that everything is ready together . . . in no time!

2. You can keep your side dishes warm by putting them on the warming rack of your grill, if you have one, or in a 200°F. oven until the main course is ready.

3. Watching your fat intake? Spray the **cold** grill racks with regular or flavored nonstick vegetable cooking spray, and grill your veggies and potatoes right on the grill. They're tasty and have little or no fat!

127

From Garden to Grill

"Steak Out" Veggies

6 servings

We all love sautéed mushrooms, and when they top our favorite steaks, we've got a double lip-smackin' treat!

½ cup olive oil
¼ cup balsamic vinegar
1 teaspoon garlic powder
1 teaspoon salt
½ teaspoon pepper
1 large red onion, cut into chunks
1 pound mushrooms, sliced

Preheat the grill to medium-high heat. In a large bowl, combine the olive oil, vinegar, garlic powder, salt, and pepper, and whisk until blended. Toss in the onions and mushrooms and let stand for 10 minutes. Place the vegetables in an 8-inch square disposable aluminum pan, put it on the grill, and close the grill cover. Cook for 8 to 10 minutes, or until the onions are tender, tossing them halfway through the cooking.

NOTE: This is perfect for topping Hot Striped Steak (page 89). Wow! Pile 'em on and eat 'em up!

Maple-Grilled
Sweet Potatoes

4 to 6 servings

Sweet potatoes add a special touch to any meal, so why not grill them along with the rest of the meal?

½ cup maple syrup
½ cup pineapple juice
¼ cup honey
4 large sweet potatoes, peeled and cut
into ½-inch-thick slices

In a large saucepan, combine the maple syrup, pineapple juice, and honey. Add the sweet potato slices and bring the mixture to a boil over medium heat on the stove top. Reduce the heat to low and simmer for 12 to 15 minutes, or until the potatoes are just fork-tender. Preheat the grill to medium-high heat. Drain the potatoes and place on the grill, reserving the sauce. Grill the potatoes for 4 to 6 minutes, or until browned, turning them over frequently and basting them with the remaining liquid.

NOTE: You can cook these potatoes and keep them in the refrigerator, covered, for up to 2 days before you plan to grill them. Then follow the directions for grilling as above.

Striped Herbed Tomatoes

4 to 6 servings

Who says tomatoes only belong on salad? Hot off the grill, these'll have your gang chanting for more!

4 large tomatoes
½ teaspoon dried oregano
½ teaspoon dried thyme leaves
½ teaspoon garlic powder
1½ teaspoons olive oil

Preheat the grill to medium-high heat. Cut the ends off the tomatoes, then cut them into ¾-inch-thick slices. Combine the remaining ingredients in a small bowl; mix well. Coat the tops of the tomato slices with the mixture. Grill the tomatoes for 5 to 7 minutes, or until heated through, turning them over once after 2 minutes. Serve immediately.

NOTE: Do not overcook these or they'll become very soft and make a mess on your grill!

No-Bake Baked Beans

4 to 6 servings

Here's a simple way to doctor up canned baked beans and have everybody thinking you made them from scratch ... and without even lighting the oven!

2 cans (16 ounces each) vegetarian baked beans
¼ cup firmly packed brown sugar
2 tablespoons ketchup
¼ cup bacon bits

Preheat the grill to medium heat. Combine all the ingredients in an 8-inch square disposable aluminum pan. Mix well and cover tightly with aluminum foil. Place the pan on the grill for 7 to 10 minutes, stirring occasionally, until the beans are bubbly and heated through.

NOTE: Not barbecuing today? No problem. This will work cooked in a saucepan over medium heat for 8 to 10 minutes, or until hot.

Foil-Baked Potatoes

4 servings

Since you're already grilling your main course, why not let some potatoes share the grill, too? It's no more work, and your house will be cooler in the summer if you don't have to light the oven!

4 medium to large red or white potatoes
½ cup (1 stick) butter, softened
¼ teaspoon salt
¼ teaspoon pepper
½ teaspoon ground cumin
½ teaspoon dried dillweed
½ teaspoon dried parsley flakes

Preheat the grill to medium-high heat. Wash the potatoes and wrap each one tightly in aluminum foil. Place the wrapped potatoes on the grill, close the grill cover, and cook for 50 to 60 minutes, or until tender to the touch, turning them over occasionally. Remove the potatoes from the grill and carefully open the foil; make a lengthwise cut three quarters of the way through each potato. In a small bowl, combine the remaining ingredients; mix well. Place a dollop on the top of each potato and serve immediately.

NOTE: Baked potatoes by themselves (without butter) contain no fat, so cooking them on the grill and having them plain is an easy way to eat smart.

Summer Salsa Veggies

4 to 6 servings

If you're like me and can never find the right side dish when you're grilling, look no further!

1 package (10 ounces) frozen corn, thawed
1 package (10 ounces) frozen cut green beans, thawed
1 teaspoon minced garlic (2 to 3 cloves)
⅔ cup medium salsa

Preheat the grill to medium-high heat. Combine all the ingredients in an 8-inch square disposable aluminum pan; mix well and cover tightly with aluminum foil. Close the grill cover and cook for 7 to 10 minutes, or until the mixture is heated through and the vegetables are tender-crisp.

NOTE: If you like your veggies spicy, then a dash of hot pepper sauce will really perk these up!

One, Two, Three Eggplant

4 to 5 servings

C'mon, let's enjoy eggplant in some recipe other than Eggplant Parmigiana (which I happen to love, too). This is a nice, light change of pace . . . and it's done one, two, three!

1 teaspoon garlic powder
½ teaspoon dried basil
1 teaspoon salt
¼ teaspoon pepper
1 medium-sized eggplant, cut into ½-inch-thick slices
½ cup olive oil

Preheat the grill to medium-high heat. In a small bowl, combine the garlic powder, basil, salt, and pepper. Brush both sides of the eggplant slices with the olive oil. Place the eggplant slices on the grill and sprinkle half of the spice mixture over them. Grill for 5 minutes. Turn the eggplant slices and sprinkle with the remaining spice mixture. Continue grilling the eggplant for another 5 minutes, or until fork-tender.

NOTE: I think this works better when the eggplant isn't peeled, because the skin helps it keep its shape while cooking.

Home-Style Roasted Peppers

3 to 4 servings

We love 'em, but we always thought they were too much work. Well, try these and I bet you'll be as surprised as I was the first time I made them this way.

2 tablespoons vegetable oil
¼ teaspoon onion powder
¼ teaspoon garlic powder
¼ teaspoon salt
¼ teaspoon pepper
4 to 5 red and green bell peppers, seeded and quartered
(about 4 cups)

Preheat the grill to medium-high heat. In a medium-sized bowl, combine all the ingredients except the peppers; mix well. Add the peppers to the bowl and toss to coat well. Place the peppers on the grill for 8 to 10 minutes, turning them over once during grilling.

NOTE: If you like your peppers crispy, then leave them on the grill a few extra minutes.

Caramelized Onions

3 to 4 servings

My family begs me to make this recipe whenever I light up the grill. I'm happy to do it 'cause there's nothing to making them, and they go with almost anything else I'm grilling!

1 pound (about 4 medium-sized) onions,
peeled and cut in half
6 tablespoons (¾ stick) butter or margarine, melted
2 tablespoons brown sugar
⅛ teaspoon salt

Preheat the grill to medium-high heat. Place the onions in a medium-sized bowl and set aside. Combine the remaining ingredients in a small bowl, mixing well until the sugar dissolves. Pour the mixture over the onions, tossing to coat evenly. Wrap the onions in heavy-duty aluminum foil and seal all the edges tightly. Place the foil package on the grill, seam side up, and grill the onions for 20 to 22 minutes, until tender and caramelized, carefully turning over the entire foil package occasionally.

NOTE: Be careful not to pierce the foil when rotating these on the grill.

137

Summer Grilled Zucchini

4 to 6 servings

In the summer our local farmers sure do produce lots of zucchini, which means it's a great buy. Let's cook up some of that value right on our grills!

¼ cup white vinegar
¾ teaspoon salt
½ teaspoon pepper
1 teaspoon dried tarragon
½ cup mayonnaise
3 medium-sized zucchini, cut in half lengthwise
1 slice Swiss, Muenster, or mozzarella cheese (optional)

In a small saucepan, combine the vinegar, salt, pepper, and tarragon, and bring to a boil. Remove the mixture from the heat and let cool. Preheat the grill to medium-high heat. Add the mayonnaise to the cooled mixture and blend well, until smooth. Brush the mixture on both sides of the zucchini slices. Grill the slices for 5 minutes on each side, with the grill cover closed. If adding cheese, top the zucchini with the cheese for 1 to 2 minutes before the cooking is completed. Cook until the cheese has melted.

NOTE: If you have some really large zucchini, I recommend using 2 and cutting them lengthwise in thirds.

138

Dilly Carrots

4 servings

Ahh, sweet carrots. They sure are one of my everyday favorites, especially after they've been rubbed with some herbs and finished on the grill. (I love 'em even more!)

¼ cup vegetable oil
½ teaspoon dried dillweed
½ teaspoon salt
⅛ teaspoon pepper
4 medium-sized carrots, peeled and cut into large sticks

Preheat the grill to medium heat. In a medium-sized bowl, combine all the ingredients except the carrots; mix well. Add the carrots to the bowl and toss with the spice mixture. Lay the carrots across the grill rack and cook for 10 to 12 minutes, or until tender, turning them over often.

NOTE: Make sure you cut your carrot sticks large enough so that they won't fall through the grill rack into the fire.

Broccoli Under Cover

6 to 8 servings

These are easy to make at the same time as you're grilling your main dish. They have a nice oniony flavor, so go ahead and steam your broccoli (and other veggies) on the grill. You'll be glad you did!

1 envelope (from a 2.4-ounce package) dry onion soup mix
½ cup water
2 heads broccoli, cut into florets (about 6 cups)

Preheat the grill to medium-high heat. In a large bowl, combine the soup mix and the water; toss with the broccoli. Wrap the broccoli in heavy-duty aluminum foil and seal tightly. Grill for 10 minutes, or until desired tenderness. Open the foil carefully to allow the steam to escape before serving.

NOTE: Other vegetables can be done this way, too, like zucchini, yellow squash, and carrots. So why not mix and match to make your family's own favorite blend?

Potatoes on a Stick

6 to 8 servings

Lickety-split—these are done! Yup, because finishing canned potatoes on the grill gives you great, long-cooked taste.

8 wooden or metal skewers
¼ cup vegetable oil
½ teaspoon salt
¼ teaspoon white pepper
½ teaspoon ground cumin
1 tablespoon paprika
2 cans (15 ounces each) whole white potatoes, drained

If using wooden skewers, soak them in water for 15 to 20 minutes. Preheat the grill to medium-high heat. In a medium-sized bowl, combine the oil, salt, pepper, cumin, and paprika; mix well. Add the potatoes and toss to coat evenly. Place the potatoes on the skewers, reserving any oil mixture. Grill the potatoes for 5 to 7 minutes, turning them over occasionally and basting with the reserved oil mixture.

NOTE: Be sure to use tongs and oven mitts when removing the skewers from the grill. If using metal skewers, be careful because they'll be hot!

141

Husky Grilled Corn

6 ears

Native Americans cooked their corn right in the husks over an open fire, and I think their idea is still the best. There's no better way to enjoy that rich, fresh-roasted taste.

6 ears of fresh corn, in the husks
½ cup (1 stick) butter, melted
Salt to taste
Pepper to taste

Place the ears of corn (still in the husks) in a large pot of cold water and soak for 1 hour. Preheat the grill to medium-high heat. Remove the corn from the water and wrap each ear (still in the husk) in a piece of heavy-duty aluminum foil. Place the wrapped corn on the grill rack and cook for 18 to 22 minutes, or until the kernels are tender. **Carefully open the foil and remove the corn, then remove the husks and silk from the corn.** Serve with the melted butter, salt, and pepper.

Sweet Endings

You ate lots of munchies and a filling main course with yummy grilled side dishes, and you're stuffed! But something tells me that you just might have a little room left for an awesome dessert straight off the grill. Not only is it a "Sweet Ending" to your meal, but it's a fun way to end the afternoon or evening before putting out the fire. So keep dessert light or pile it high—whichever way ends your grilling with a smile and, of course, an **"OOH it's so GOOD!!™"**

P.S. It's a good idea to clean your grill with a grill brush (see page xxvii) before putting your Sweet Endings on it. After all, you wouldn't want your Striped Citrus Pound Cake (page 146) or Waffle Sundaes (page 151) to come off the grill tasting like Mustardy Pork Chops (page 107), Crusted Salmon (page 114), or whatever else you just made!

Sweet Endings

Chocolate-Stuffed Bananas

4 to 6 servings

It's like a banana dipped in chocolate fondue—without all the work or cleanup! My mouth waters just thinking about the great taste.

6 firm bananas, unpeeled
½ cup semisweet chocolate chips

Preheat the grill to medium-high heat. Make a lengthwise slit (about three quarters of the way through) down the center of each banana and stuff it with chocolate chips. Wrap each banana tightly in aluminum foil. Grill the bananas for 10 to 12 minutes, or until the chocolate chips are slightly melted. Unwrap the bananas and remove the skins. Slice the bananas into 2-inch pieces and serve immediately.

NOTE: Since these can be a little messy, you might want to serve them with toothpicks, or slice them a little smaller and serve over ice cream.

Striped Citrus Pound Cake

8 to 10 servings

You'd better put on your sunglasses when you serve these, 'cause they're so colorful—and such a great summer right-off-the-grill quick dessert.

1 10¾-ounce frozen pound cake
2 cans (11 ounces each) mandarin oranges, drained,
with juice reserved
1 package (3 ounces) orange-flavored gelatin mix
2 tablespoons butter or margarine
Whipped cream for topping

Cut the pound cake into ¾-inch-thick slices (about 8 to 10 slices). Place the reserved mandarin orange juice in a medium-sized saucepan. On the stove top, heat the juice to almost boiling, over medium-high heat. Add the gelatin mix, reduce the heat to low, and stir until the gelatin is dissolved. Add the butter and stir until melted. Brush some of the mixture onto one side of each cake slice. Preheat the grill to medium heat. Place the slices on the grill, brushed side down. Brush the other sides and grill for 5 to 6 minutes, turning and brushing occasionally, until the cake slices are heated through. Remove the slices to serving plates and top with the oranges and whipped cream.

146

Grilled Grapefruit

4 servings

My favorite way to eat grapefruit used to be right from the fridge, but after experimenting with a few slices on the grill, I think I've changed my mind!

3 large grapefruit
1 tablespoon sugar
½ teaspoon ground cinnamon

Preheat the grill to medium-high heat. Slice the ends off the grapefruit. Cut ¾-inch-thick rounds, yielding about 3 to 4 slices per grapefruit. In a small bowl, combine the sugar and cinnamon. Sprinkle both sides of the grapefruit with the cinnamon and sugar mixture. Grill the grapefruit for 5 to 6 minutes, or until the grapefruit slices are hot and the sugar begins to caramelize, turning the slices over halfway through the cooking.

Campfire S'mores

8 sandwiches

After cooking up lots of grilled favorites, how 'bout finishing off your meal with a favorite from the days when we all sat around the campfire telling ghost stories?

8 wooden or metal skewers
8 large marshmallows
2 milk chocolate candy bars (1.45 ounces each)
8 graham crackers, split in half

If using wooden skewers, soak them in water for 15 to 20 minutes. Preheat the grill to medium-low heat. Place a marshmallow on the end of each skewer. Break the chocolate bars into 4 pieces each and place 1 piece on each of the 8 graham cracker halves. Carefully hold the skewered marshmallows over the grill until the marshmallows begin to turn golden, about 3 to 4 minutes. When the marshmallows are done to your liking, top each piece of chocolate with a marshmallow, then another graham cracker half, making sandwiches. Serve immediately.

NOTE: When I was growing up, we speared our marshmallows with sticks. Skewers are definitely a better choice 'cause they don't add that authentic woodsy taste of tree bark!!

Banana Bake

6 servings

We bake potatoes, we bake squash, cakes, casseroles, even fish. So why shouldn't we "bake" bananas—right on the grill?!

1 teaspoon ground cinnamon
¼ cup sugar
6 firm bananas, unpeeled

Preheat the grill to medium-high heat. In a medium-sized bowl, combine the cinnamon and sugar. Place the unpeeled bananas on the grill for 20 minutes, turning them over once. (The skin will turn almost black.) Carefully remove the bananas from the grill, peel, and slice. Toss the slices in the cinnamon and sugar mixture. Serve immediately.

NOTE: I suggest serving these with a selection of dipping sauces, like hot fudge, butterscotch topping, warm maple syrup, and honey. It's like a make-your-own-banana bar!

Tutti-frutti Shortcake

6 to 8 servings

Sometimes after a big barbecued meal, you feel like a light-tasting, summery dessert—and this combination is just the trick!

1 can (16 ounces) fruit cocktail, undrained
2 tablespoons brown sugar
½ teaspoon ground cinnamon
1½ teaspoons cornstarch
¼ cup cold water
1 16-ounce pound cake, cut into 1-inch-thick slices

Preheat the grill to medium heat. In a disposable 8-inch square aluminum pan, combine the fruit cocktail (with its juice), brown sugar, and cinnamon; mix well and set aside. In a small bowl, dissolve the cornstarch in the water. Place the fruit mixture in the aluminum pan on the grill and heat through, stirring occasionally. When hot, add the cornstarch mixture and mix until it starts to bubble and thicken slightly, about 5 to 7 minutes. Place the pound cake slices on the grill to warm, if desired (about 2 minutes per side). Remove the cake to a serving platter and spoon the fruit mixture onto the pound cake slices.

NOTE: No fruit cocktail on hand? Go ahead and use a 16-ounce can of peaches or pears instead.

150

Waffle Sundaes

8 sundaes

Waffles right off the grill? You betcha! And with our favorite toppings, they go from a breakfast winner to an eyebrow-raising dessert treat in a snap.

1 tablespoon butter or margarine
⅓ cup maple or pancake syrup
8 frozen waffles
1 pint ice cream, any flavor
1 cup chocolate-flavored syrup
1 container (8 ounces) frozen whipped topping, thawed

Preheat the grill to medium-high heat. In a small saucepan on the stove top, melt the butter with the maple syrup. Baste both sides of the frozen waffles with the maple syrup mixture. Grill the waffles for 2 to 3 minutes on each side, or until crisp and lightly browned. Place the waffles on plates and top with ice cream, chocolate syrup, and whipped topping.

NOTE: You can even top these with Chocolate-Stuffed Bananas (page 145).

Grilled Walnut Topping

6 to 8 servings

Old-fashioned ice cream parlors used to serve a topping like this one called Wet Nuts and boy, oh boy, were they good! Bring back those tasty memories by using your grill and just a few ingredients.

½ cup sugar
1 teaspoon ground cinnamon
2 egg whites
1 tablespoon water
2 cups shelled walnut pieces
1 cup maple or pancake syrup

Preheat the grill to medium heat. In a small bowl, combine the sugar and cinnamon; mix well and set aside. In a medium-sized bowl, combine the egg whites and water. Add the walnuts, mixing to coat them evenly. Add the cinnamon and sugar mixture and stir to coat evenly again. Place the mixture in an 8-inch square disposable aluminum pan. Grill for 7 to 9 minutes, mixing often, until the nuts and sugar begin to brown. Mix in the maple syrup and heat thoroughly. Remove from the grill and cool slightly before serving over ice cream.

NOTE: The walnuts get very hot, so be careful! Make sure they cool slightly before handling them or putting them over ice cream.

Hot Hawaiian Pineapple Slices

8 to 10 slices

There's something about heat that brings out the sweetness in fruit. And if we add a little extra zing, pineapple can really satisfy the biggest sweet tooth!

10 maraschino cherries (from a 16-ounce jar), drained,
with 1 cup juice reserved
½ cup orange juice
¼ cup firmly packed brown sugar
1 fresh pineapple, peeled and sliced
into ½-inch-thick rounds

In a small bowl, combine the 1 cup cherry juice, the orange juice, and brown sugar; mix well. Add the pineapple slices, cover, and refrigerate for 2 hours, or overnight. Preheat the grill to medium-high heat. Grill the pineapple slices for 6 to 8 minutes, or until slightly softened, turning them over halfway through the cooking. Serve the pineapple slices garnished with the cherries.

NOTE: This makes a great light dessert, and it's also a perfect "go-along" for poultry or pork.

Patriotic Apple Pie

6 servings

Grilling is certainly American, and so is apple pie. Why not team them, and together they'll add up to one really patriotic dessert!

¼ cup (½ stick) butter or margarine
4 cups peeled, thinly sliced baking apples
(about 4 medium-sized apples)
½ cup granulated sugar
¼ cup firmly packed brown sugar
⅓ cup crushed gingersnaps
½ teaspoon ground cinnamon
1 teaspoon cornstarch
6 single-serving graham cracker tart shells

Preheat the grill to medium-high heat. In a large cast-iron or other heavy skillet with a heat-proof handle, melt the butter on the grill and sauté the apples until almost tender. In a small bowl, combine the sugars, crushed gingersnaps, cinnamon, and cornstarch; sprinkle the mixture over the apples. Cook for 2 to 3 minutes, stirring, until a thick dark sauce forms. (Depending on the juiciness of the apples, you may need to stir in 1 to 2 teaspoons of water to thin the sauce.) Remove the mixture from the heat and spoon it into the tart shells. Serve warm or chill until ready to use.

NOTE: When removing the skillet from the heat, use a pot holder and **be careful—the handle gets mighty hot**. These "pies" can be served plain or topped with whipped cream or scoops of frozen yogurt, custard, or ice cream.

Index

Index

Mr. Food®

Can Help You Be A Kitchen Hero!

Let **Mr. Food**® make your life easier with

Quick, No-Fuss Recipes and Helpful Kitchen Tips for

Family Dinners   *Soups and Salads*   *Pot Luck Dishes*
Barbecues   *Special Brunches*   *Unbelievable Desserts*

...and that's just the beginning!

There are easy, updated versions of Mama's specialties in **Mr. Food**® Cooks Like Mama, new twists on American classics in **Mr. Food**® Cooks Real American, and scrumptious treats in **Mr. Food**® Makes Dessert and **Mr. Food**® 's Favorite Cookies. And now, with the incredibly simple **Mr. Food**® 's Quick and Easy Side Dishes, the barbecuing bonanza in **Mr. Food**® Grills It All in a Snap, and the gold mine of helpful hints in **Mr. Food**® 's Fun Kitchen Tips and Shortcuts (and Recipes, Too!), **it's all here!** All of **Mr. Food**®'s recipes use readily-available ingredients, and can be made in no time! So, don't miss out! Join in on the fun!

It's so simple to share in all the
OOH IT'S SO GOOD!!™

TITLE	PRICE	QUANTITY		
. **Mr. Food**® Cooks Like Mama	@ $12.95 ea.	x _____	=	$_____
. The **Mr. Food**® Cookbook, OOH IT'S SO GOOD!!™	@ $12.95 ea.	x _____	=	$_____
. **Mr. Food**® Cooks Chicken	@ $ 9.95 ea.	x _____	=	$_____
. **Mr. Food**® Cooks Pasta	@ $ 9.95 ea.	x _____	=	$_____
. **Mr. Food**® Makes Dessert	@ $ 9.95 ea.	x _____	=	$_____
. **Mr. Food**® Cooks Real American	@ $14.95 ea.	x _____	=	$_____
. **Mr. Food**®'s Favorite Cookies	@ $11.95 ea.	x _____	=	$_____
. **Mr. Food**®'s Quick and Easy Side Dishes	@ $11.95 ea.	x _____	=	$_____
. **Mr. Food**® Grills It All in a Snap	@ $11.95 ea.	x _____	=	$_____
. **Mr. Food**®'s Fun Kitchen Tips and Shortcuts (and Recipes, Too!)	@ $11.95 ea.	x _____	=	$_____

Book Total $_____

Send payment to: **Mr. Food**®
P.O. Box 696
Holmes, PA 19043

**+$2.95 Postage & Handling *First Copy* AND
$1 Ea. Add'l. Copy
(Canadian Orders Add
Add'l. $2.00 *Per Copy*)** $_____

Name_____

Street_____

Subtotal $_____

City_____State_____Zip_____

Less $1.00 per book if ordering 3 or more books with this order $-_____

Method of Payment: ☐Check or Money Order Enclosed

☐ Credit Card: ☐ Visa ☐ MasterCard: Expiration Date _____

Add Applicable Sales Tax (FL Residents Only) $_____

Signature_____

Total in U.S. Funds $_____

Account #:

☐☐☐☐☐☐☐☐☐☐☐☐☐☐☐☐

Please allow 4 to 6 weeks for delivery.   BKI1